Praise for *Think Like a Feminist*

"A timely and accessible introduction to feminist thought in the twenty-first century. Highly recommended."
—Ásta, author of *Categories We Live By: The Construction of Sex, Gender, Race, and Other Social Categories*

"Carol Hay is a warm and witty guide through modern-day gender politics, welcoming novices and offering substance to those already with her in the trenches. This is the book to give the questioning young person or the cynical patriarch in your life, but also a good read for your feminist book club or radical action group."
—Alice MacLachlan, editor, *Feminist Philosophy Quarterly*

"With this book, beautifully written and often disarmingly hilarious, we see clearly the luminous future for feminism, and one of its brightest lights will be Carol Hay."
—Clancy Martin, professor of philosophy, University of Missouri–Kansas City

"At once welcoming and inclusive, yet uncompromisingly political, Carol Hay recognizes the wide variety of feminist voices while speaking boldly in a voice of her own."
—Quill R. Kukla, professor of philosophy, Georgetown University

"The best feminist work leaves you changed, unable to look at the world in the same way. *Think Like a Feminist* does this. Carol Hay provides historical perspective, political awareness, and philosophical insight to cut through confusions about feminism, giving us the tools of analysis and skills of engagement needed to build a more just world."

—Sally Haslanger, Ford Professor of Philosophy and Women's and Gender Studies, Massachusetts Institute of Technology

"*Think Like a Feminist* has opened my eyes in ways I had not known they were closed. It is a timely and deeply important book, and I cannot recommend it highly enough, especially for those who yearn for justice for all human beings, no matter their sex, gender, or race." —Andre Dubus III

THINK
LIKE
A
FEMINIST

THINK LIKE A FEMINIST

THE PHILOSOPHY BEHIND THE REVOLUTION

CAROL HAY

W. W. NORTON & COMPANY
Independent Publishers Since 1923

A version of some of the arguments in Chapter 4 first appeared in an article I
published in the *New York Times*, "Who Counts as a Woman," April 1, 2019.

A version of some of the language at the end of Chapter 5 first appeared in an
article I published on Daily Nous, "Enabling the Sociopathy No More,"
November 21, 2017.

For information about permission to reproduce selections from this book, write to
Permissions, W. W. Norton & Company, Inc., 500 Fifth Avenue, New York, NY 10110

For information about special discounts for bulk purchases, please contact
W. W. Norton Special Sales at specialsales@wwnorton.com or 800-233-4830

Manufacturing by Lakeside Book Company
Book design by Chris Welch
Production manager: Lauren Abbate

Library of Congress Cataloging-in-Publication Data

Names: Hay, Carol, 1977– author.
Title: Think like a feminist : the philosophy behind the revolution / Carol Hay.
Description: First edition. | New York, NY : W. W. Norton & Company, [2020] |
Includes bibliographical references and index.
Identifiers: LCCN 2020010917 | ISBN 9781324003090 (hardcover) |
ISBN 9781324003106 (epub)
Subjects: LCSH: Feminist theory. | Feminism.
Classification: LCC HQ1190 .H396 2020 | DDC 305.42—dc23
LC record available at https://lccn.loc.gov/2020010917

ISBN 978-1-324-02027-1 pbk.

W. W. Norton & Company, Inc., 500 Fifth Avenue, New York, N.Y. 10110
www.wwnorton.com

W. W. Norton & Company Ltd., 15 Carlisle Street, London W1D 3BS

1 2 3 4 5 6 7 8 9 0

FOR BECCA

CONTENTS

PREFACE

Something has changed.

Only a few years ago, we found ourselves collectively able to live with those who would explain away the "locker-room talk" of the man who would go on to become the president of the United States. The progressive catharsis of the Women's Marches was threatening to go pretty much nowhere, fizzling out while pussy-hats and safety pins went from de rigueur to passé in a matter of months. Politicians merrily continued chipping away at women's right to have sex without a permission slip from our creepy Uncle Pence. Working women patiently plodded along, eagerly anticipating the closing of the gendered pay gap by 2119.

But then, seemingly out of nowhere, the accretion of male sins became impossible to ignore. We hit a tipping point, and suddenly so many of us were sharing our stories. The MeToo movement has laid bare the elephant in the room, skeletons burst from closets, dirty laundry flaps in the breeze. Hollywood actresses have banded together to announce that "Time's Up," and they've done it in conjunction with the workers' rights activists and organizers who've been at this stuff for decades. Not a day seems to go by without another high-profile allegation being offered up to the court of public opinion, where we jurors are asked to pass judgment on cases with sometimes sketchy access to the facts and an even sketchier understanding of the moral or legal theories that might help us make sense of things. After centuries of progress coming at a snail's pace, things are now shifting too quickly for anyone to figure out what the hell is going on.

This book presents a long-view take on women's reckoning with sexual harassment and sexual assault by putting these concerns into a larger historical and sociopolitical context, framing them in terms of the battles that feminists have been waging for hundreds of years.

I'm an academic philosopher. This means that my scholarly writing is usually read by about nine other people, most of whom share my intellectual and political commitments and want merely to quibble over the details. Even when the scholarly debate gets fierce it usually remains civil; even when disagreement is genuine it usually remains impersonal. But over the years I've come to learn that when you go public with your opinions, the debate doesn't always remain so civil. A few years ago, for example, I published an op-ed where I argued that our culture simply doesn't know how to deal with women in positions of authority because until fairly recently it didn't have to. I thought the essay expressed a fairly uncontroversial position, one that merely laid out a century of very careful work in social and political philosophy for a general audience. Female professors, I claimed, have a particularly difficult time establishing a rapport with students that doesn't revolve around the tired tropes of saintly mother or sexual plaything, neither of which are terribly pedagogically useful.

When Sigmund Freud argued that women could be seen as Madonnas or whores, he didn't get hate mail. His was considered an objective treatment of the subject. Mine, apparently, was not, and the hate mail just kept coming: I was immature. A neurotic. "I feel sorry for her children," readers said. "I feel sorry for her students. For her husband." Much of the negative feedback I received in the wake of this op-ed amounted to the accusation that I was a narcissistic whiner tilting at windmills. The restrictive roles that women are forced to play in our culture aren't *that* bad, I was told, and they certainly don't amount to oppression. "Grow up and deal with it," one reader wrote. "If a student acts inappropriately, slap him or her down and get on with being a professor."

Similar admonitions have been lobbed at today's proponents of MeToo. "Apparently there is a whole country full of young women who don't know how to call a cab," Caitlin Flanagan snarked.[1] Dave Chappelle took aim at the woman who charged his friend Louis CK with masturbating in the middle of a telephone call, calling her "weak" and chiding: "Bitch, you don't know how to hang up a phone?" Katie Roiphe griped, "It feels as if the feminist moment is, at times, providing cover for vindictiveness and personal vendettas and office politics and garden-variety disappointment, that what we think of as purely positive social change is also, for some, blood sport. The grammar is better in these feminist tweets, but they are nonetheless recognizably Trumpian."[2] Comparable sentiments have been expressed by opinionati across the political spectrum: that the MeToo movement has predictably descended into hysteria, that red-blooded men are now presumed guilty until proven innocent, that we've raised a generation of pearl-clutching politically correct snowflake prudes who've fetishized the victimization of women and are going to ruin sex by taking all the hot, messy ambiguity out of it.

Are these critics right to claim that some women are using this cultural moment to overreact or accuse men who are innocent? Of course they are. But the concern-trolling calls for due process, and the blanket insinuations that everyone who's hopped on the MeToo bandwagon has abandoned it, are unfair and unhelpful. Selling out your purported allies as fringe and extreme while portraying yourself as the only one with sense in a conversation has, sadly, become a standard move in the lefty playbook. (The left is frighteningly good at cannibalizing itself.) We can admit that not every woman who has helped herself to the MeToo hashtag is perfect—that some have overreacted, that others have made unintentional mistakes, that others are bad actors willing to use the movement for selfish and immoral purposes in order to ruin the lives of innocent men—without accepting the charge that these few bad apples undermine the credibility of the rest of us.

The MeToo movement raises some big questions: Where does this movement fit into the larger history of feminist theory and activism? What exactly are feminist theory and activism? Why are they necessary in the first place? I wrote *Think Like a Feminist* for anyone who wants to go beyond the present moment and better appreciate the foundations on which MeToo and other comparable social movements rely.

As it turns out, there's a very long history of feminist thought available to be brought to bear here. *Think Like a Feminist* will show how feminism rejects a framework that analyzes things only at the level of individual personal responsibility. It'll show how sexism functions like the wires in a birdcage: how seemingly small and disconnected problems can in fact be interconnected and mutually supporting. It'll make sense of the seeming paradox that there are morally important distinctions to be made between clumsy flirtation and sexual assault, but that these behaviors are also not unrelated.

Flying in the face of the stereotype of feminists as manhaters, a major theme in the pages that follow will be women's own culpability in this mess. I'll explain why there are often very good reasons for women to go with the flow, and why it's often very difficult to do otherwise. This is, in part, because it's next to impossible to avoid internalizing society's expectations about what women are supposed to want and how we're supposed to act. But when we unquestioningly participate in a system that harms people, then we share in the responsibility for perpetuating that system. I'll argue that women should take responsibility for the roles we play that entrench a system that harms not only us but all other women. But I'll also argue that we should cut ourselves and other women a whole lot of slack, because we need to appreciate just how monumental the system we're up against is. Each of us is just trying to make it to tomorrow.

Think Like a Feminist explains why men in general are not the enemy here, but rather an interconnected system of sexist norms, habits, expectations, and institutions. Many of these things function well below the level of conscious awareness, and most implicate women as well. I try to be honest about the mistakes feminists have made in the past—about how our calls for solidarity among women far too often gave in to the temptations of racism, classism, ableism, homophobia, or transphobia. While mostly focusing on the ideas behind and history of feminist activism, I also have some practical advice to share about how to start cleaning up this mess. Along the way, I promise to turn the stereotype of the humorless feminist bitch on its head, introducing you to some of the central lessons of feminist theory in a manner that is accessible, unintimidating, and as amusing, irreverent, and undidactic as possible.

You'll need to permit me a degree of polemicism, however: purporting to present the definitive take on *anything* is a fool's bargain, much less a topic as varied and controversial as feminism. I promise to do my very best to present as many of feminism's strands as possible, and I'll try to avoid getting bogged down in its internecine battles, but I won't pretend to be neutral about which iterations of feminism I prefer or that all are equally valid. For instance, I think TERFs (trans-exclusionary radical feminists) are feminists who don't deserve the name—no one should get to call herself a feminist if she doesn't care about all women, and trans women are women. I think incidents like Susan B. Anthony declaring, "I will cut off this right arm of mine before I ever work or demand the ballot for the Negro and not the woman," or Betty Friedan scaring up a "lavender menace" to disassociate the feminist movement from LGBTQ causes, are black marks on the movement's history that still haven't been properly made up for.

In writing *Think Like a Feminist*, I'm drawing on more than twenty years of experience teaching and writing about feminist theory. I'll introduce readers to the key ideas developed by women (and the occasional man) throughout history who have refused to accept the status quo, thinkers who've known the importance of understanding why women have been getting the short end of the stick for-basically-ever and have a few ideas about what needs to be done about it. Having spent a very long time playing Whac-A-Mole with people's misconceptions of feminism—in the classroom, on social media, at the Thanksgiving dinner table—I've ended up with a whole bag full o' tricks to get the skeptics' guard down and get them to listen to what feminism is really about. This book is the collection of this hard-won repertoire. I'll point out why combatting the oppression of women will take more than hashtags, more than pussyhats, more than "leaning in." I'll show why we need to pay attention to the history of the feminist movement, both its successes and its failures. And I'll lay out the astounding variety of feminist thought that's available today, thanks to new ideas about gender, sex, and sexuality.

THINK
LIKE
A
FEMINIST

CHAPTER 1

THE F-WORD

Feminism has a PR problem. If I had a dollar for every time I heard someone say, "I'm not a feminist, but . . ." and then go on to say all sorts of explicitly feminist things, I could close the wage gap single-handedly. Half the people I meet think feminists are scary man-hating harpies who just need to get laid. The other half think feminism amounts to vacuously affirming every choice a woman makes on no other grounds than that someone with two X chromosomes is pulling the trigger. Neither of these misconceptions accurately represents the movement, but it's worth spending some time with them to get a sense of just how broad the spectrum is of what feminism means today. Before we get there, we'll take a quick look at some speculations on where sexism comes from and a brief history of the feminist movement that has arisen in response.

But first, a working definition of feminism might be helpful. Unfortunately, a completely precise and tight definition is pretty hard to come by. Honestly, if you were to ask ten feminists to define feminism you'd probably get eleven different answers. There are a few core things that we do agree about, though. First, feminists agree that women have been, and continue to be, disadvantaged relative to men. According to almost every metric that exists to measure people's quality of life—health, wealth, political participation and representation, security and freedom, subjective reports of happiness, and so on—women don't fare as well as men. Second, feminists agree that these disadvantages are bad things that can and should be changed. And third, we agree that these disadvantages are interrelated, that they're the result of mutually supporting systems of privilege and deprivation that are structurally embedded in virtually every aspect of society and that systematically function to screw women over. That's pretty much it, in a nutshell: *Just a basic recognition of well-established facts about women's realities that are backed up by most historians and social scientists on the planet, plus some kind of sense that this situation isn't the best and maybe we should do something about it, plus some kind of realization that this isn't a problem that can be tackled piecemeal.* As we'll see, though, other than agreeing on this single fact, this single moral belief, and this single interpretive lens, feminists can disagree about almost everything else.

The feminist movement is messy, rife with internal disputes and contradictions, and as varied as the women it represents. Despite what the conservative pundits might have you believe, there is no feminist agenda—there simply isn't enough we agree on to ground a single shared course of action. If anything, there are multiple, sometimes competing, feminist agendas.

The Origins of Sexism

Before we take a deep dive into feminism's historical and theoretical underpinnings, it's worth asking how, exactly, we got here in the first place. Why do we need feminism? At what point did the boys start taking all the good stuff for themselves? The origins of patriarchal sexism predate recorded history, so to some degree we're in the realm of anthropological speculation here. A fairly plausible just-so story comes from John Stuart Mill, a nineteenth-century British philosopher and social theorist (and one of the few men to have made substantive contributions to feminist theorizing). "From the very earliest twilight of human society," Mill lamented in 1869, "every woman (owing to the value attached to her by men, combined with her inferiority in muscular strength) was found in a state of bondage to some man."[1] We're basically looking at a situation of *might makes right*, Mill conjectured: laws arose to sanction the relations of dominance and submission that existed because men had the physical ability to force women to obey them. These laws and other formal social institutions maintain male dominance even though we now live in a world where physical power has virtually nothing to do with social power.

Shulamith Firestone, a radical feminist activist and author of the 1970 book *The Dialectic of Sex*, pointed elsewhere to explain the origins of sexism. Rather than attributing inequality between the sexes to differences in muscular strength, Firestone blamed the biological differences between men's and women's roles in reproduction.[2] Because women bear children, and because until very recently we didn't have access to birth control that lets us decide whether and when to have kids, we've historically been at the mercy of our biology in ways that men haven't. This was exacerbated by the fact that until the relatively recent invention of infant formula, we were also the only source of food for babies, and therefore their natural caregivers. Firestone, like Mill, pins the blame for women's inequality on biology, but she argues that the sexes' different roles in childbearing and -rearing gave rise to a division of labor that systematically burdened women.

A similarly biological explanation for inequality between the sexes comes from evolutionary psychology. According to its standard narrative, men are aggressive and promiscuous and seek to ensure the survival of their genes by impregnating as many fertile young women as possible, while women are passive and chaste and try to pass on their genes by manipulatively trapping a mate who will use his physical strength to protect her and her offspring. In the words of prominent evolutionary psychologist David Buss, "At this point in history, we can no longer doubt that men and women differ in their preferences for a mate: primarily for youth and physical attractiveness in one case, and for status, maturity, and economic resources in the other."[3] Males are driven to father as many offspring as there are fertile females willing to mate with them, and will try to control one or several females in order to increase their certainty of paternity so that they're not wasting energy protecting some other man's kids. Females, in turn, are limited in the number of offspring they can bear and are thus choosy about whom they mate with, mustering all of their manipulative powers to rope in a protective male. Evolutionary psychologists believe that these different reproductive strategies result in deep psychological, behavioral, and physical differences. As glossed memorably in the early 1990s by the pop psychologist and self-help author John Gray, men are from Mars, women are from Venus. Men are supposed to be fundamentally aggressive, territorial, violent, logical, emotionally cool, socially dominant risk-takers; women are empathetic, compassionate, communicative, emotional, cautious, scheming nurturers. That these reductive lists of character traits conveniently map onto tired old gender stereotypes whose origin could just as likely be social as biological doesn't seem to strike many evolutionary psychologists as meriting a second thought. Nor do they seem very bothered by the fact that these purported differences between the sexes aren't morally neutral: they make men more likely to dominate women and women less likely to resist this domination. Evolutionary psychologists shrug at these assumptions of social order, with perhaps too little concern about whether they're overstating the differences between the sexes, understating the similarities, not acknowledging historical changes that allow babies to be raised by either sex, and ultimately hawking ideologically driven stereotypes dressed up as disinterested scientific fact.

It's grim fun to speculate about where male dominance comes from, to imagine ourselves back into the lives of cavemen and hunter-gatherers. It's even fun to occasionally entertain the theories of evolutionary psychologists (only occasionally, though, because some of them are fantastically good at using pure speculation to justify a regressive status quo). But at the end of the day this line of inquiry probably isn't the most useful. Where sexism comes from is ultimately irrelevant; what we really care about is if it can and should be changed. And the answer to these two questions, one that I and generations of feminists before me have been committed to fighting for, is a resounding *yes*.

A Brief History of Feminism

As the history of Western feminist theory and activism is usually told, we should think of the movement as progressing in waves. The story runs from the nineteenth century's "first wave" of feminism and its successes in securing certain political and legal rights for many women, through the twentieth century's "second wave" of feminism that realized that these formal rights weren't nearly enough to secure a flourishing life for all women, to today's "third wave" of feminism that recognizes that women's concerns have too often been misunderstood as, and limited to, affluent white women's concerns. This is the story I'm about to lay out for you, more or less. But it's a story that needs to be told with a few caveats. One problem with this wave metaphor is that it can obscure the very diverse strands of activism and the internal disputes that took place within each of these movements. Another is that it tends to mistakenly imply that there's been a linear march of feminist progress, that the successes of one wave have been steadily built on by those of the next with no backlash, backsliding, inconsistencies, or partial victories. But the battles of all three waves are still being fought or defended in different parts of the world.

THE FIRST WAVE

The story begins with the eighteenth-century social critic Mary Wollstonecraft, whom I, like many others, credit with having "invented" feminism.* When she wrote *A Vindication of the Rights of Woman* in 1797, the oppression to which women were subjected was obvious: women couldn't vote; they couldn't easily divorce, own property, hold public office, go into business or the professions, inherit family estates, access information about birth control, or speak their mind in the public square. When Wollstonecraft wrote her tract on behalf of women's rights, the intellectuals of her time mocked her, arguing that if rights were extended to women then they might as well be granted to pigs and dogs. Thankfully, the first-wave feminists who followed persevered, overcame such atrociously bad arguments, and went on to secure the vote and other basic political rights and legal protections in the coming two centuries. Philosophers like John Stuart Mill and Harriet Taylor Mill wrote treatises defending women's right to full participation in the public sphere. Activists like Margaret Sanger and Emma Goldman went to jail for daring to distribute information about birth control. Social reformers like Jane Addams revolutionized our understandings of how to

---

* Fun fact: Wollstonecraft was the mother of Mary Shelley, the author of *Frankenstein*. There's probably a joke about feminism being the stuff of some people's nightmares there somewhere....

tackle poverty. Suffragists like Elizabeth Cady Stanton, Susan B. Anthony, Alice Paul, and Lucy Burns devoted their lives to winning women's suffrage—which didn't happen in the United States until 1920.* Labor reformers like Frances Perkins and Mary McLeod Bethune lobbied against racial discrimination and unsafe working conditions for women and children.

Ironically enough, many historians think the word "feminism" was actually coined by a man—by Charles Fourier, a philosopher and utopian socialist writing in France at the beginning of the nineteenth century.[4] None other than Karl Marx would claim intellectual indebtedness to Fourier's conviction that all people are entitled to a "social minimum" of fulfilling work and adequate food, clothing, shelter, and entertainment, and his recognition that work could be communal, pleasant, and assigned according to preference and skill.[5] But it was Fourier's willingness to extend his insights to women as well as men that's earned him a spot in the history books. "As a general proposition," Fourier claimed, *"Social progress . . . [is] brought about as a result of the progress of women toward liberty; and the decline of social orders is brought about as a result of the diminution of the liberty of women. . . . To sum up, the extension of the privileges of women is the general principle of all social progress."*[6] Many of the feminist suggestions in his fantastical utopian vision for society sound shockingly progressive even to contemporary ears. Fourier believed that people shouldn't be channeled into occupations on the basis of their gender, proposing that children between the ages of one and three be dressed and raised alike so their true talents would have a chance to emerge over those that are conventionally

---

* Wrap your head around this: women have been voting in this country for *less than 100 years.*

imposed. He criticized the institution of marriage for oppressing women by condemning them to a life of conjugal servitude that deprived them of both economic and sexual fulfillment. Because women were typically prohibited from most forms of employment, Fourier lamented that "prostitution more or less prettied up is their only resort."[7]

Fourier was writing in a time of tremendous social upheaval, a time when beliefs championing women's equality were very much in the air. The first self-proclaimed *"féministe"* was Hubertine Auclert, who used the term to refer to herself and her fellow French suffragists in 1882. The term *"féminisme"* was being regularly used to refer to activism for women's equality by the 1890s, migrating from French and entering the English language as early as 1894.[8]

Influenced by the liberal political ideals of liberty and equality that characterized the Enlightenment in general, first-wave feminists argued that because women have the same rational capacities as men they deserve the same rights. The central goals of this phase of the movement were equal political rights and economic opportunities for women. First-wave feminism's major successes included women's suffrage (the right to vote); the right to own property; reproductive freedoms, such as the right to access information about birth control; and access to education and some professions.

THE SECOND WAVE

Despite all this progress, the victories of feminism's first wave were at best partial. Many of its political and legal successes didn't extend to women from more marginalized groups, didn't encompass enough inequalities, and did little to address the cultural factors that restrict the lives of women. Rosie the Riveter might have successfully encouraged women to join the war effort, but the instant WWII was over the same middle-class women who'd been told it was their patriotic duty to dirty their hands in factories were told it was their womanly duty to give those jobs back to the men who truly deserved them.* Second-wave feminists realized that securing only formal equalities for women meant that many effects of sexism had been left untouched. French existentialist philosopher Simone de Beauvoir published *The Second Sex* in 1949, sparking a conversation that continues to this day among feminists about how the forces of socialization oppress women. Feminist theorists following in her wake would go on to explore how sexist oppression infects not just the *formal* economic, political, and social arrangements that first-wave feminism had challenged, but also *informal* norms, habits, everyday interactions, and social institutions, such as marriage, motherhood, and heterosexual relationships. And newfound reproductive freedoms—thanks to the introduction of the contraceptive pill in 1960 and the legalization of abortion in 1973—let women, for the first time in history, escape the specter of unwanted pregnancy and exercise more control over their lives.

Betty Friedan's bestselling 1963 book *The Feminine Mystique* argued that even the seemingly mundane details of women's personal lives, such as "the problem that has no name"—the dissatisfaction shared by many middle-class housewives—could be the appropriate subject of moral and political analysis. "The problem," Friedan wrote, "lay buried, unspoken, for many years in the minds of American women. It was a strange stirring, a sense of dissatisfaction, a yearning that women suffered in the middle of the 20th century in the United States. Each suburban wife struggled with it alone. As she made the beds, shopped

---

* Marxist feminist economists argue that women function as a "reserve army of labor"—workers who can be called in and out of the labor force as dictated by the needs of the economy, their own needs or desires be damned.

for groceries . . . she was afraid to ask even of herself the silent question—'Is this all?'"[9] These suburban housewives began to form afternoon coffee hours and evening drinking groups organized for the purpose of "consciousness-raising."

Second-wave feminism's major successes included women's increased participation in the public sphere; expanded reproductive freedoms such as access to improved birth control methods and to safe and legal abortions; important changes to custody and divorce laws and the laws against domestic and sexual violence; and improvements in the general public's beliefs about women's equality. But, once again, some women were better able to reap these benefits than others.

A rift began to open up within the feminist movement, between those who were focused primarily on improving the lot of women who were privileged enough to have the time and energy to engage in the self-help and self-improvement that characterized many consciousness-raising groups, and those focused on the well-being of women who were still struggling for much more basic social rights and recognition. Some radical feminists, claiming that "Feminism is the theory, lesbianism is the practice," advocated lesbian separatism—considering all cooperation and contact with men, including heterosexual sex and marriage, to be collaborating with the patriarchy.* Other feminists, such as Friedan, saw lesbian activism as a distraction, labeling lesbians a "lavender menace" and attempting to push them out of mainstream feminist causes. Many women of color were more easily aligned with civil-rights groups like the Black Panthers than with white feminists, although they often found themselves restricted to subservient or supportive roles

---

* The slogan's original source is unclear; it has been ascribed both to Ti-Grace Atkinson and the Chicago Women's Liberation Union.

in those organizations.* Black feminist writers and activists critiqued the second wave's ideal of an easy sisterhood between women who lived very different lives, urging feminists to look at the different challenges that women face in terms of class, race, and sexuality.

THE THIRD WAVE

Feminism's third wave was officially ushered in by the writer and activist Rebecca Walker, who wrote in *Ms.* magazine in 1992—in the wake of Clarence Thomas's controversial confirmation hearings, which pitted the black feminists defending Anita Hill against both the black activists decrying the racism in the proceedings and the white feminists who were oblivious to it— declaring that "to be a feminist is to integrate an ideology of equality and female empowerment into the very fiber of life. It is to search for personal clarity in the midst of systemic destruction, to join in sisterhood with women when often we are divided, to understand power structures with the intention of challenging them. . . . I am not a postfeminism feminist. I am the Third Wave."[10] Third-wave feminism's realizations—that the history of feminism is also a history of racism and classism, that the status quo is usually willing to let a few token women rise through the ranks as long as they don't rock the boat and upset the power structures that keep everyone else subjugated, that there are a lot of women who have it a great deal worse than the relatively

---

* Writing of her experiences dealing with the sometimes brutal sexism of the Black Panthers, Elaine Brown writes, "A woman in the Black Power movement was considered, at best, irrelevant. A woman asserting herself was a pariah. If a black woman assumed a role of leadership, she was said to be eroding black manhood, to be hindering the progress of the black race. She was an enemy of the black people." Brown, *A Taste of Power: A Black Woman's Story* (New York: Pantheon Books, 1992), 357.

privileged white women who have historically been at the helm of the feminist movement—continue to offer necessary course corrections.

These uncomfortable realities have been available to feminists for centuries—seen, for example, in the escaped slave Sojourner Truth's famous 1851 "Ain't I a Woman?" speech:

> That man over there says that women need to be helped into carriages, and lifted over ditches, and to have the best place everywhere. Nobody ever helps me into carriages, or over mud-puddles, or gives me any best place! And ain't I a woman? ... I could work as much and eat as much as a man—when I could get it—and bear the lash as well! And ain't I a woman? I have borne thirteen children, and seen most all sold off to slavery, and when I cried out with my mother's grief, none but Jesus heard me! And ain't I a woman?*

If feminists of color have been shouting into the wind for centuries, it took feminism's third wave for the importance of their ideas to finally start getting the uptake they deserved. Third-wave feminists continue to remind us that as long as we continue to make the experiences of cis,† white, straight, middle-class, able-bodied women central to the feminist cause, we still won't have come up with an adequate response to Truth's question.

In this same vein, decolonial feminist philosophers, such as

---

* Most historians now agree that this well-known version of Truth's speech likely differed considerably from what she actually said in 1851. This transcription, published by Frances Gage in 1863, gave Truth speech characteristics of Southern slaves that she, born and raised in New York, almost certainly didn't have.

† If you're cisgender—"cis" for short—the gender with which you identify matches up with the sex assigned to you at birth.

Chandra Mohanty, Uma Narayan, and Alison Jaggar, criticize the tendency of many Western feminists to treat women from the Third World as if they were one homogenous group whose members face identical oppressive harms.[11] Narayan calls out our proclivity for treating these women as if their agency has been "pulverized by patriarchy."[12] We're perfectly capable of seeing ourselves as struggling to do the best we can within the constraints of what our society deems acceptable for us—bemoaning the fact that we can't get ahead in business unless we don pantyhose and high heels, grudgingly dyeing the grays from our hair, blowing paychecks on overpriced face creams to maintain the illusion of our perpetual youth, or submitting to the tortures of Spanx and push-up bras—but then we see a brown woman from an impoverished country wearing a hijab and decree that she must be either a "dupe" or a "prisoner" of an oppressive worldview. Much of the work in postcolonial feminism has been influenced by a landmark essay by the literary theorist Gayatri Spivak called "Can the Subaltern Speak?" In it, Spivak characterizes colonialism as a mission of "white men saving brown women from brown men."[13] In this context, Western feminism can start to look like "white women saving brown women from brown men."

Decolonial feminists argue that hundreds of years of racism and colonialism have given us in the West a superiority complex that can make it difficult for us to realize that Third World women are very likely doing what Narayan calls "bargaining with patriarchy" just as much as we are. We see a burkini and tut-tut about how tragic it is that the woman wearing it can't properly enjoy a hot day at the beach, never stopping to consider that our swimwear options are just as constrained by the male gaze. What performances of femininity are acceptable, how much skin we're permitted to display, how to avoid or cultivate or channel men's lust: these are minefields that virtually every woman on the planet must negotiate. The point here isn't to pretend that women from the Third World aren't victims of sexism, it's that people in glass houses shouldn't throw stones. If we're going to criticize the cultural practices of others, we need to make completely certain we're equally willing to cast scrutiny on our own.

In many ways, the current MeToo movement is a recapitulation of second-wave feminist consciousness-raising. It provides a chance for women to contribute their experiences to a growing list of problematic cultural practices and social mores that still govern the lives of half the world's population. This movement, however, should be in a better position than the second-wave feminists of the 1960s through the '80s. With any luck we've managed to learn a few things in the interim. The term "me too" wasn't, at least at first, a hashtag. It wasn't invented by the white actress Alyssa Milano. "Me Too" was a slogan invented by a black woman—Tarana Burke—who ran a nonprofit in the 1990s to help victims of sexual assault. It can be far too easy to forget this—that sexism and its resistance don't just have to do with wealthy white actresses and their Twitter followers. This is the message of third-wave feminism: that sexism and racism and other forms of oppression like classism (discrimination against people of lower socioeconomic status) and ableism (discrimination against people with disabilities) and homophobia and transphobia are always interconnected, and as long as we continue to ignore these relationships we'll only ever advance the interests of some women at the expense of others.

The following chapters will explore ideas from all three of feminism's waves. But before diving into what feminism is, we need to talk about what feminism *isn't*. There are at least two caricatures that get traction in the popular imagination these days—the Angry Feminist and the Girl Power Feminist. What these misconceptions have in common is that each, in their own way, leaves the status quo untouched.

Angry Feminism

If feminism is just a bunch of irrationally angry bra-burning lesbians who want to castrate men and confiscate women's makeup and high heels, then it's a caricature we don't need to take seriously. But it's a caricature with legs—hairy ones, at that. The Angry Feminist does hair all wrong: too much on her legs and armpits and face and vulva, not enough on her head. Sporting a weird dykey haircut, combat boots or Birkenstocks, and way too much plaid, she drinks her coffee out of a mug labeled MALE TEARS.*

Angry Feminists elevate man-hating to an art form. Their agenda is laid out most clearly by Valerie Solanas, author of the controversial *SCUM Manifesto* and Angry Feminist par excellence:† "Life in this society being, at best, an utter bore and no aspect of society being at all relevant to women, there remains to civic-minded, thrill-seeking females only to over-throw the government, eliminate the money system, institute complete automation and destroy the male sex."[14] More suc-cinctly, in the words of antifeminist televangelist Pat Robertson, Angry Feminism "encourages women to leave their husbands, kill their children, practice witchcraft, destroy capitalism and become lesbians."[15]

Then, while stomping about in a state of perpetual rage, the Angry Feminist has the nerve to turn around and get offended by literally everything men say. She's a nagging social justice warrior who gets inexplicably furious when all you were try-

---

* I own this mug.
† Solanas self-published the *SCUM Manifesto* in 1967, then unsuccessfully attempted to murder Andy Warhol in 1968. Rejected by the mainstream femi-nism of the day, she spent the rest of her life on the margins of society, but her work would go on to inspire generations of radical feminists.

ing to do was hold the door open for her, who can't tell "men's desire for achievement and competence" apart from "a patriarchal desire for tyrannical power."[16] She's a victim-mongering prude who views every man as a proto-rapist presumed guilty until proven innocent. Too ugly to merit anything other than pity sex, she resents men for rejecting her and subverts her jealousy of the pretty women men do want into a sour-grapes rejection of feminine beauty standards. Whether you're a fashionista or a stay-at-home mom or simply a woman who happens to be sexually attracted to men, the Angry Feminist makes it 100 percent clear that she's judged you and your life choices and found them wanting.

This stereotype of feminists is so aggressively unpleasant that it tends to put off men and women alike.

Men are appalled by the specter of the Angry Feminist because they've been told it's their birthright to have women make their lives more pleasant. From mothers who kiss their scraped knees to girlfriends who laugh at their jokes and submit to reenactments of degrading porn scripts to secretaries who deliver coffee to wives who pick up where their mothers left off and single-handedly shoulder the responsibility of making sure no one in the household runs out of clean underwear or dies of scurvy, women's job is to make the world harmonious for men. If the whole point of women is to cater to men's needs and whims, then Angry Feminists are basically impossible to grok as women. Men hate these feminazis for calling into question centuries of unchallenged entitlement, for casting suspicion on the legitimacy of their red-blooded desires, for the unforgivable suggestion that traditionally gendered divisions of emotional and material labor are unfair. Because it refuses to play the man-pleasing game, Angry Feminism—abrasive, judgmental, unaccommodating, unpleasant—is dangerous. If the Angry Feminist can convince enough other women to join her, then the jig is up. Better to write her off, if at all possible, as a nasty woman who can't take a joke.

Women, on the other hand, are horrified by Angry Feminists because our training in the care and feeding of men has been so thoroughgoing that we often don't see our servile behavior for what it is. We just know that we're deathly afraid of being taken for one of those harpies. "Many women," speculates the radical feminist activist Andrea Dworkin, "resist feminism because it is an agony to be fully conscious of the brutal misogyny which permeates culture, society, and all personal relationships."[17] It's more fun to indulge the inconsistent and fickle delights permitted us by the norms of femininity than to admit that these norms exist primarily for the amusement and benefit of men. It's easier to fight other women over the scraps than to admit to ourselves that we are sometimes quite literally in bed with the enemy, that the men we love are implicated in, benefit from, and sustain the very world order that keeps us from living fully flourishing lives. It's safer to lie to ourselves than admit that, when all is said and done, we serve at the pleasure of those we love.

Simone de Beauvoir ushered in what would come to be known as the second wave of feminism by taking up the question of why so many women succumb so willingly to men's rule. In explaining why women had not collectively resisted their oppression, de Beauvoir suggested that women acquiesce because to do otherwise would be to renounce the few advantages they do get from their oppressive relationships with men. Acquiescing not only affords many women some degree of financial support, it also allows them to avoid taking existential responsibility for their lives. De Beauvoir understood that living an existentially authentic life—one in which each and every one of your choices is completely free, and completely yours—can be arduous, even terrifying. Most people, existentialists tend to believe,

are cowards, preferring to avoid at all costs the terrors of deciding for themselves what their lives will be about. But making
self-defining choices is what existentialists take to be distinctive of an authentic human existence. Social roles in general are
existentially problematic, they believe, because they make these
self-defining choices for people inauthentically. But women's
socially prescribed gender roles are particularly problematic,
de Beauvoir argues, offering women even fewer opportunities
than men to make existentially authentic choices. When women
take on the role of wife or mother, for example, their lives tend to
become defined entirely by their relationships to their husbands
or their children. These women lose their sense of self, becoming what de Beauvoir calls an "Other." But being an Other can be
considerably less formidable than carving out for oneself a life
that has value and meaning.

> To decline to be the Other, to refuse to be party to
> the deal—this would be for women to renounce all the
> advantages conferred upon them by their alliance with the
> superior caste. Man-the-sovereign will provide woman-
> the-liege with material protection and will undertake the
> moral justification of her existence; thus she can evade at
> once both economic risk and the metaphysical risk of a
> liberty in which ends and aims must be contrived without
> assistance. Indeed, along with the ethical urge of each
> individual to affirm his subjective existence, there is also
> the temptation to forgo liberty and become a thing. This
> is an inauspicious road, for he who takes it—passive, lost,
> ruined—becomes henceforth the creature of another's will,
> frustrated in his transcendence and deprived of every
> value. But it is an easy road; on it one avoids the strain
> involved in undertaking an authentic existence.[18]

De Beauvoir condemns this gendered failure to take existential responsibility as a form of cowardice, championing those women brave enough to reject the conventional gender roles that lead them down this path. But these days, a mere whiff of the suggestion that the roles available to women might be inferior to what's open to men tends to instigate yet another skirmish in the now-tedious Mommy Wars, bolstering the emergent stereotype of Angry Feminism as hostile to stay-at-home moms and anyone else with "traditional" values.

As we'll see, de Beauvoir and those in her wake are almost always less interested in passing judgment on what individual women choose to do with their lives than in taking on the social structures that constrain women's options in the first place. But skeptics fasten onto the image of the Angry Feminist as a sanctimonious shrew who should mind her own business because it's less unsettling to muster outrage over her ungrounded right to criticize what you've done with the hand you've been dealt than it is to sit with the possibility that she might be right when she claims that the deck's been stacked.

In a heteronormative culture like ours, one in which a woman's primary source of power too often hinges on whether she's considered to be attractive to men, the Angry Feminist is profoundly *unsexy*. Because our value hinges on whether men find us agreeable, women hit our prime early and can then anticipate a lifetime of watching our power fade with our youthful beauty. Meanwhile, because men's stock consists primarily of their earning power, it usually continues to rise well into middle age and beyond, dad bods and all. (In my thirties I dated a guy who would joke that when I turned forty he intended to trade me in for two twenty-year-olds. Sensing that he probably wasn't entirely joking, I didn't stick around long enough to find out.) Given the snowballing power imbalance we have to look forward

to, women are hardly to be faulted for making a rational calcula-
tion to invest in our feminine charms in the service of locking
down the most eligible bachelor willing to put a ring on it.

Philosopher Sandra Bartky identifies a deep sense of pride,
self-worth, and competence that women who are capable of mas-
tering the requirements of femininity can gain. Women recognize that feminine beauty is highly prized in our culture. A
woman who's capable of living up to the standards of feminine
beauty stands to garner real benefits, and real power, at least as
long as she's able to play the game. (And, of course, zillion-dollar
industries lie in wait to capitalize on her horror of the inevitability of aging out.) When Angry Feminism questions whether all
this work is worth it, it imperils women with what Bartky wryly
identifies as "a certain de-skilling."[19] A woman who's spent a
lifetime internalizing and trying to adhere to a particular aes-
thetic standard of beauty could be forgiven for her reluctance
to abandon it for someone else's lofty political ideals. Insofar as
feminism aims to do away with conventional understandings of
masculinity and femininity, Bartky speculates that many women
might see it as endangering their sexuality, their identity, their
very sense of what the social world is like (and their place in it).

Whatever else there is to be said of the perennial pain in the
feminist rear that is Camille Paglia, she understands the allure
of femininity. "We should not have to apologize for reveling in
beauty," she scolds. "Beauty is an eternal human value. It was not
a trick invented by nasty men in a room someplace on Madison
Avenue."[20] In Paglia's view, women's sexual allure is responsible
for nothing short of the entirety of human civilization. Because
every work of human genius is male, she argues, women's roles
in the creative process are that of muse or of reward. We feminists are lying to ourselves when we refuse to admit that it can be
intoxicating to play this role, Paglia thinks. It's absurd to pretend
that the only thing that could motivate a woman to invest so much

time and energy in her performance of femininity is a deluded failure to appreciate her true worth. Paglia isn't wrong about this at least: those of us willing and able to stage this performance successfully know how blood-tingling it can be, for even the briefest of moments, to see the desire in the eyes of a lover (or a stranger) and know that you've made them want you. Angry Feminism is a big old wet blanket in this context, grasping its pearls over a sexual dynamic that is likely as old as human culture itself.

What's more, women understand, on some level, that men have the bulk of the power in our society. Most of the time, then, our only real chance at having a slice of the pie depends on whether men can be convinced to share. And men are most likely to share their power with women who are willing to give them something they want—be it flattery, sex, emotional support, offspring, or domestic labor. Women are thus extremely incentivized to play nice.

The perceived danger of Angry Feminism, then, is that it threatens to rob women of what little power we have in a status quo that exists by and for the benefit of men. Women sour on this kind of feminism because we see feminists as enemies of glamor, because we resent being called out for our failures of existential responsibility, because we think it threatens what little influence we have in a man's world. If we can write the Angry Feminist off as crazy, we don't have to recognize that the focus of her anger is usually not individual people but the background social structures in which choices are made. And, what's more, we don't have to consider the possibility that this anger might actually be legitimate.

And this possibility deserves to be taken very, very seriously.

Fasten your seat belts. In 1995, a black woman boarded a Boeing 747, took her seat next to a white man in a suit, and wrote an essay that begins by confessing, "I am writing this essay sitting beside an anonymous white male that I long to murder." A lifetime of black womanhood—with all its attendant humiliations and injustices—had led her to this culminating moment. "We have just been involved in an incident," she explains, "where K, my friend and traveling companion, has been called to the front of the plane and publicly attacked by white female steward-esses who accuse her of trying to occupy a seat in first class that is not assigned to her." Unwilling to admit that it had mistak-enly assigned the same seat to both K and the anonymous white guy, the airline's only priority was ensuring that the white man would not be denied his seat in first class. Unwilling to admit his complicity with the racism and sexism pervading the situ-ation despite being willing to admit that "no white man would have been called on the loudspeaker to come to the front of the plane while another white male took his seat," the anonymous white guy offered an "insincere, face-saving apology," insisted that the situation "was not his fault," and made clear he felt he should be left alone "to sit back and enjoy his flight." "I stare him down with rage, tell him that I do not want to hear his liberal apologies," the author writes. "I felt a 'killing rage.' I wanted to stab him softly, to shoot him with the gun I wished I had in my purse. And as I watched his pain, I would say to him tenderly 'racism hurts.'"[21]

The woman who wrote this is the celebrated author, feminist, and social activist bell hooks. And my oh my, is she *angry*. But her murderous anger makes sense when it's put into proper per-spective. She points out that for all our culture's insistence on characterizing women and people of color as fundamentally emotional (as opposed to white men being fundamentally rea-sonable), anger is the one emotion these people aren't permitted. Why? hooks has figured out something the rest of us need to get on board with: anger has the ability to upset the status quo in a way that no other emotion can.

Too often, we use a woman's anger as an excuse to avoid listening to what she has to say. Recounting an incident that is likely familiar to many, the black feminist theorist Audre Lorde writes, "I speak out of direct and particular anger at an academic conference, and a white woman says, 'Tell me how you feel but don't say it too harshly or I cannot hear you.' But is it my manner that keeps her from hearing, or the threat of a message that her life may change?"[22] Identifying herself as a "feminist killjoy," the feminist theorist Sara Ahmed defends the political potency of righteous anger. We live in a world where women are trained to make nice. We're trained to avoid upsetting other people at all costs. We're trained to be aghast at the thought that we've made other people unhappy. We're trained to think happiness should be the ultimate goal for ourselves as well. But happiness in a world that is corrupt, in a world that is brutally unjust, can be a lie. Insisting on happiness when there is nothing to be happy about can be a way of refusing to perceive reality. We need to let ourselves be angry sometimes. "To be involved in political activism," writes Ahmed, "is to . . . be involved in a struggle against happiness."[23] By refusing to make happiness our political cause—by being willing to make others unhappy, by being willing to support others who cause unhappiness, by being willing to be unhappy ourselves—we open up the possibility of making political change.

But allowing ourselves to get angry can be a terrifying prospect. "For women raised to fear, too often anger threatens annihilation," writes Lorde. "In the male construct of brute force, we were taught that our lives depended on the good will of patriarchal power. The anger of others was to be avoided at all costs because there was nothing to be learned from it but pain, a judgment that we had been bad girls, come up lacking, not done what we were supposed to do."[24] This training in what emotional responses are acceptable for people like us, instilled early on, can be difficult to unlearn.

But properly harnessed, anger can be a powerful source of change. Author Rebecca Traister argues that even though women's anger "has often been the sparking impetus for long-lasting, legal, or institutional reform," too often this fury has been scrubbed from the record books.[25]

> We aren't taught that Rosa Parks, the perfectly demure woman whose refusal to give up her seat kicked off the Montgomery Bus Boycott in 1955, was a fervent antirape activist who once told a would-be attacker that she'd rather die than be raped by him and who, at ten years old, threatened by a white boy, picked up a piece of brick and drew it back to strike him if he approached. "I was angry," she'd later say of that youthful act of resistance. "He went his way without further comment." We are never forced to consider that rage—and not just stoicism, sadness, or strength—were behind the actions of the few women's heroes we're ever taught about in school, from Harriet Tubman to Susan B. Anthony. Instead, we are regularly fed and we regularly ingest cultural messages that suggest that women's rage is irrational, dangerous, or laughable.[26]

This history of angry women is one we'd do well to remember, and to embrace.

The abhorrence of Angry Feminism explains why it's a favorite target of those looking to discredit the feminist movement in general. It's a stereotype that spins women's well-founded anger over legitimate grievances into the age-old specter of the irrational hag whose wailings needn't be taken seriously. But people who are actually open to feminism often flock to another caricature, one that's problematic for different reasons. If Angry Feminists' sin is that of being unlikeable women, Girl Power Feminists are determined not to be tarred with the same brush.

Girl Power Feminism

The Girl Power Feminist is sexy, feisty without being off-putting, and fundamentally unthreatening. She's confident without being pushy. She proclaims her independence but promises not to do anything too radical with it. Girl Power Feminists are often professionally and financially successful—they lean in at work, they capitalize on the platitudes they've heard since childhood assuring them that girls can do anything, they assume everyone else can do the same. Understanding women's empowerment as the success of individual women, not the collective betterment of all women, Girl Power Feminism claims a victory every time a woman makes it in a man's world. Corporate women's leadership events are Girl Power Feminism. "Girls Rule, Boys Drool" is Girl Power Feminism. Beyoncé performing without pants in front of a giant screen emblazoned with the word "FEMINIST" is Girl Power Feminism. (Beyoncé in other manifestations is almost certainly more than this, it must be said.) The Spice Girls practically invented the genre. Anyone who makes money selling an uncritical fantasy of a feel-good sisterhood is likely a Girl Power Feminist. Anyone who makes money selling a conception of female beauty that congratulates itself on its "inclusivity" or "diversity" is probably a Girl Power Feminist. Anyone who makes money hocking self-help platitudes that celebrate women's intuition and self-empowerment is in all likelihood a Girl Power Feminist. This kinder, gentler feminism talks the talk of championing women's empowerment, but it does so without ruffling feathers, reassuring everyone that the status quo won't be interrupted in any significant way.

It's no coincidence that the statue that faced down the bull on Wall Street is a Fearless Girl, not a Fearless Grown Woman. Strength in girls is unthreatening precisely because they're still too little to actually do anything with it; strength in women is off-putting as hell. Girl Power is marketing gold. Woman Power, not so much. When Fearless Girl leans in, it's cute and spunky. When real women lean in, they face untold disappointments and uphill battles—even Facebook exec Sheryl Sandberg recanted her optimism after the untimely death of her husband, admitting in a Facebook post that she "did not really get how hard it is to succeed at work when you are overwhelmed at home." We're a culture that's happy to inspire little girls with tales about how they can do anything, but far less interested in accommodating the adult women who are trying to make this a reality for themselves. There's a telling disparity between the qualities men say they're looking for in a wife or partner and what they hope for in their daughters: according to the Shriver Report, the same men who value qualities like "strength," "intelligence," and "independence" in daughters apparently turn around and say they most want a wife who is "attractive" and "sweet."[27] I guess those dads think a daughter's feistiness should be someone else's problem?

Another face of Girl Power Feminism manifests in a kind of unreflective sex positivity. In 2011 and 2012, for example, we saw a spate of "Slutwalks"—protests responding to ongoing sexual violence against women—whose supporters announced they were reclaiming the word "slut" as part of their demands for women's right to control and revel in their sexuality. Don't get me wrong, I'm as much in favor of securing the sexual freedoms for women that men have always enjoyed as any other red-blooded human being. And if sex positivity manages to help women feel good in their bodies, or to move beyond men's ideas about what makes a woman attractive, it stands to help feminism move forward. But as Traister points out, it can be hard not to see the most palatable versions of Girl Power's sex positivity as "traffick[ing] in a kind of winking, eroticized irony"—as cool, campy, in-jokes whose main purpose seems to be to assure men that girls still "just wanna have fun."[28] Echoing this idea, author Ariel Levy criticizes much of today's sex positivity as amounting to a "raunch culture" intent on selling women the lie that it's empowering to internalize objectifying views of themselves and other women.[29] Both authors see this sex positivity as less a radical feminist renunciation of unfair sexual double standards than a response to the work of radical feminists like Catharine MacKinnon and Andrea Dworkin, who showed themselves willing to form coalitions in the 1980s with conservative politicians to pass legal ordinances to restrict access to pornography that they deemed a violation of women's civil rights. "I'm a radical feminist," Dworkin famously quipped, "not the fun kind."[30]

Girl Power Feminists run screaming in the opposite direction. This version of feminism makes inroads by reassuring straight men that whatever parts of the status quo Girl Power Feminism might take issue with, men's unrestricted sexual access to women and right to get laid pretty much whenever they want isn't on the chopping block. It's meant to reassure us, if you will, that its proponents are anything but Angry Feminists guilty of Paglia's infamous charge that "Leaving sex to the feminists is like letting your dog vacation at the taxidermist's."[31]

If feminism is just Girl Power, then we don't need to look at the larger social structures that undergird individual women's choices, nor do we need to consider the possibility that women are often complicit in maintaining sexism. Women aren't stupid. We're not deluded. We rightly recognize that what little power we have in a man's world is contingent on our not rocking the boat. Girl Power Feminism lets us ignore the fact that, so much the worse for the sisterhood, there are often real rewards available to women who are willing or able to go along with what a sexist society expects from them.

The kind of soul-searching required to be completely honest with ourselves about the ways we're complicit in a system that ultimately harms us, along with all other women, isn't easy. Girl Power Feminism lets us ignore all this depressing rumination by celebrating acts by individual women. It lets us pretend that all that feminism asks is that we champion women's right to make their own decisions. It lets us avoid considering that women are often choosing from an extremely constrained set of options, at least when compared to what's open to men. And it lets us avoid taking a hard look at what it is that women are actually choosing. But as philosopher and lawyer Linda Hirshman points out, hiding behind the rhetoric of choice is often just an attempt to not defend your decisions.[32] Girl Power Feminism's blinkered focus on the individual means we don't have to admit that our individual choices might be reinforcing a male-dominated world order.

If what I choose to do with my life negatively affects what you're able to do with yours, you have legitimate grounds for complaint. But in our neo-liberal consumerist culture that valorizes individual freedom above all else, people don't like hearing that their choices aren't happening in a social vacuum and might have negative consequences for others in society. Chronicling what she sees as the fall of feminism from radicalism to self-help, the editor and critic Jessa Crispin sums up Girl Power Feminism as nothing more than a fight to enable women to buy their way out of the worst of the patriarchy, "a fight to allow women to participate equally in the oppression of the powerless and the poor."[33] In the ideology of Girl Power Feminism, the old feminist aphorism that "The Personal Is Political" is misinterpreted as a slogan that adorns our personal choices with political righteousness without our having to answer for their political ramifications. "For too long," writes Crispin, "feminism has been moving away from being about collective action and collective imagination, and toward being a lifestyle. Lifestyles do not change the world."[34]

Girl Power Feminism has legs, in large part, because advertising companies have figured out that it can be co-opted to get women to buy more stuff we don't need. "Women Now Empowered by Everything a Woman Does," crows a headline from the satirical news site *The Onion*, mocking the absurd notion that the point of feminism is to pat women on the back for the audacity of owning dozens of pairs of shoes or taking calcium-rich antacids or lunching in small groups with other women.[35] Feminism as self-care, as self-empowerment, as self-absorption, as marketing strategy, as lifestyle choice, is toothless. When feminism is reduced to you-go-girl banalities it's stripped of its radical potential to affect the world in meaningful ways, which is precisely why Girl Power Feminism has been absorbed so readily by the mainstream: it poses absolutely no threat to upend the social structure.

It's no coincidence that the Angry Feminist and the Girl Power Feminist get so much cultural uptake. A lot of people fear change, and a lot of people are invested in maintaining an unjust status quo that benefits them at the expense of others. Each caricature manages to defang feminism of its radical potential. But real feminism—diverse as it is—already has and will continue to change the world.

CHAPTER 2

OPPRESSION

FOUR METAPHORS

If there's one theoretical concept that's central to feminist philosophy, it's oppression. This idea, more than any other, is what's needed to make sense of a dizzying array of feminist arguments and insights. Once you grasp it, you have almost all you need to understand a feminist view on the world.

The word "oppression" is used informally in all sorts of contexts—we call everything from overly strict parents to muggy August heat "oppressive"—but for feminists oppression is a distinctive, as opposed to generic, phenomenon. Oppression is a cluster of harms and injustices forming an interconnected web made up of economic, political, social, and psychological elements. They result from a structural and systemic network of social institutions—workplace, family, education, religion, popular culture, and media—and they operate according to norms, rules, laws, and assumptions that unfairly disadvantage women while unfairly privileging men. Defining oppression this way is all well and good, but it risks being too abstract and esoteric. In my many years of introducing folks to feminist philosophy I've found that the fastest way to get up and running with this idea is through a collection of metaphors.

A birdcage metaphor highlights that the harms and injustices of oppression fundamentally affect people because of their membership in a social group. A metaphor of an invisible knapsack shows that oppressive harms and injustices are very often not the result of individual intentional action, and this affects how we should think of moral concepts like privilege and responsibility. A prison metaphor illustrates how oppression is often internalized, so that people take on the work of oppressing themselves. And a metaphor of a traffic intersection explains how oppression's effects are compounded (often in unpredictable ways) when a person is a member of multiple oppressed groups.

These metaphors, along with a handful of others, will be the primary tools in your feminist toolbox. Once you've taken them on board you'll understand why we need to analyze people's behavior not only on the level of individual choice. You'll grasp why this doesn't mean it's cool to Netflix and chill while Rome burns. You'll understand how and why women voluntarily do a lot of the patriarchy's work for it. And you'll see why the voices we're so used to granting authority to don't necessarily have the best advice for getting us out of this mess.

The Birdcage

Say one day you come across a hungry bird that's standing motionless in front of a pile of seeds. Why doesn't the bird hop over and devour the food, you ask yourself? It's literally starving, and yet there's a huge pile of seeds right in front of it. What's the bird's problem? You're staring right at it and you can't, for the life of you, figure out what's wrong. But then you step back a bit and realize there's a wire in front of the little thing. We're not talking razor wire, or electric wire, but the wire—no matter how thin— still explains why the bird doesn't hop straight forward to get its lunch: there's something in its way. Still, you can't figure out why the silly bird doesn't just hop around it. "You're seriously going to let one solitary wire, one single setback, prevent you from doing what you need to survive, Bird? Toughen up! Ever hear of a little thing called grit? Resilience? Pulling yourself up by your bootstraps? It's just one wire, right?" But then you step back a bit more and see another wire, also standing between the bird and its meal. And this one is connected to the first wire, the two of them jointly blocking a much wider swath of the bird's path than either one would be able to alone. You step back even further and see another wire. And another. And another. And finally you realize that there isn't one or two or three, but hundreds, *thousands* of wires between the bird and its food. The bird is completely constrained, its starvation virtually ensured, by a series of interconnected barriers. No one of these wires, by itself, would be capable of affecting the bird's life in any real way. But collectively, the wires completely determine what's possible for the creature.

This birdcage metaphor was first introduced by philosopher Marilyn Frye in the early 1980s, and to me it's still the best way to wrap your head around the structural and systemic nature of oppression.[1] No one wire, by itself, can constrain a bird. Similarly, no one pinch on the ass can oppress a woman. But a catcall, another catcall, a pinch, an unwanted squeeze, a patronizing look, an overlooked promotion, another pinch, a grope that goes too far, an act of chivalry that's wholly unwanted and unneeded, being called slutty if you have sex or frigid if you don't, earning 81 cents on your white male colleague's dollar (or 65 cents if you're black, or 61 cents if you're Latina),[2] being expected to give up your name in marriage, being "given away" by one man to another in a wedding ceremony, watching films that treat women like sexy furniture instead of actual people, putting up with the absurdity of straight dudes who somehow find a way to make your lesbian sexuality a performance for them, attending a church where only men get to be made in God's image, being portrayed as a hypersexualized Jezebel or spitfire if you're black or Latina or a sexually passive doll if you're white or Asian, clocking more than twice as many hours on household chores as a husband who seems to think his dinner is cooked and house is cleaned and children are tended by invisible gnomes, growing up being told in no uncertain terms that what you look like is more important than what you do or how you feel, being one of the 1 in 6 women who will experience sexual violence (or one of the 6 in 6 women who structure their lives around trying to avoid it), another pinch on the butt, being mistaken for your secretary, having to drive almost 200 miles to get an abortion you're legally entitled to—all of this, taken together, forms a cage that women cannot escape. No matter how smart or resilient or ingenious we are.

The birdcage metaphor explains why feminists sometimes seem to get their panties in a bunch over incidents that can look trivial—things like chivalry, or off-color jokes, or catcalling. It explains why we keep going on about tampon taxes, about paying twice as much as a man to dry clean a similar shirt, about the lack of good speaking roles for female actors. It explains our outsized frustration at the ubiquity of pants without functional pockets. We freak out about this stuff because we understand that, taken together, these things aren't trivial at all, that they can't be understood in isolation, that they're all connected. If most of these slights took place randomly, or in a social vacuum, it'd be like water off a duck's back: annoying, perhaps, but ultimately inconsequential. It's ridiculous to expect every social interaction to be seamless or affirming or wonderful, but properly appreciating the birdcage metaphor explains why it's unfair to claim that a woman who lets these things get to her just needs to grow a thicker skin. Collectively, the effect of individual incidents of oppression can be less like water off a duck's back and more like that of water on stone. One single drop of water isn't capable of doing anything to a rock. But collectively, the many drops in a torrential river can carve monumental valleys. Given enough time, and enough repetition, water can wear stone completely away.

And these incidents aren't really random, are they? A straight cis dude doesn't have to navigate a world where complete strangers feel entitled to comment on his physical appearance, where he's told that he'd be so pretty if only he smiled more. He doesn't have to live in a world where the threat of sexual violence looms at all times, where the outfit he's chosen to wear is taken to be evidence of whether or not he was asking for it. He didn't grow up playing with toys designed to impart the not-so-subtle message that whether he's taken to be aesthetically pleasing or domestically useful to the opposite sex is more important than just about anything else in the world. He isn't bombarded with romantic scripts that eroticize the idea of him being a victim lying around waiting to be rescued, or pornographic scripts that fetishize his objectification or humiliation. He doesn't have colleagues who undermine his professional successes by snidely suggesting that he's slept his way to the top, or alternatively write them off as the work of affirmative action rather than being deserved. He doesn't have to try to avoid internalizing the message that he deserves all this garbage.

Shit happens, right? Everyone faces random setbacks at some point in our lives: anyone can be unlucky enough to get mugged or lose their car keys or have their house carried away by a tornado. But the harms and injustices of oppression don't target people randomly, and they aren't random in their effects. Instead, certain kinds of people, and not others, are picked out to endure their brunt.

SOCIAL GROUP MEMBERSHIP

The insight that people can face harm or injustice not merely as individuals but also as members of social groups has its roots in Marxist theory. In capitalist societies like ours, Karl Marx thought, the most significant social grouping is that of socio-economic class. Which class you're a member of is determined by your relationship to society's means of production. (The means of production is basically how your society makes stuff. If you're a member of the proletariat, you're a worker who makes the stuff; if you're a member of the bourgeoisie, you're the one who actually owns the stuff and you control and exploit the workers who make it.) Oppression, for Marx, is just the ongoing exploitation of one socioeconomic class (the proletariat) by another (the bourgeoisie).

Oppression actually wasn't an especially central concept for Marx, but feminists have found the strategy of focusing on exploitative social positions to be incredibly useful in explaining power relations between the sexes. Oppression theorists' analyses have broadened beyond Marx's focus on class to encompass unjust relationships between people based on factors ranging from race to ethnicity, nationality, sexual orientation, age, body size, (dis)ability, religion, and, of course, gender. While Marx thought class relations were the fundamental drivers of inequality in society, they're now understood to be merely one of the many differences between people that are responsible for oppressive injustices. And you don't have to buy into Marx's focus on economics and his pessimism about the free market in order to accept the basic Marxist insight: *the social groups you're sorted into will have massive effects on your life and prospects.*

Carving up a social world into groups that can provide a theoretical foundation for things like self-understanding, social critique, and political solidarity is sometimes referred to as *identity politics*, but to be honest this term is used in a variety of contradictory ways and is often maligned or misunderstood. It's now gone so far out of vogue that it's difficult to find many theorists who comfortably identify their work with this label, which is more often used as a dismissive or accusatory slur (by both the right and the left). This isn't to say that this kind of theoretical analysis doesn't go on any longer. It's just one of those situations where the work chugs along but we no longer call it by the old name.

The uncontroversial insight that's central to identity politics is that some kinds of people have it a lot easier than others in our world. The slightly more controversial insight that's central to identity politics is that there are discernible patterns to these relationships of advantage and disadvantage. Society, oppression theorists believe, is made up of groups of people who are caught up in mutually reinforcing relationships of privilege and subordination. Each of us is simultaneously a member of multiple social groups, none of which come with formal membership cards but all of which collectively and heavily influence what kind of opportunities are open to us. Membership in more powerful groups makes your life go better; membership in subordinate groups makes it harder to get ahead. Sometimes we can pass as a member of a more privileged group (like when people assume we're straight, cis, white, or able-bodied when we aren't). Sometimes we can trade one group membership in for another (like when someone acquires a disability later in life, or converts to a new religion). Sometimes group membership is more or less invisible (like sexual orientation); other times it's fairly obvious from first meeting (like gender or race). Most of these memberships are unchosen (like race), but they don't have to be (like religion).

RELATIONSHIPS OF ADVANTAGE AND DISADVANTAGE

If a harm or injustice is to count as an instance of oppression, according to oppression theorists, *members of a non-oppressed group ultimately must benefit from it.* This dynamic might initially strike you as strange—how do white property owners benefit from racialized redlining, or nondisabled people benefit from buildings without elevators or ramps, or men who aren't rapists benefit from rape culture, you might ask? The advantage here can be hard to see until you recognize that *relative advantage* can function as a benefit. If members of one group face systematic hardships that members of a second group don't, then members of the second will be in a better position than members of the first to compete for limited resources, even if they're not personally responsible for the existence of these hardships. Not having to compete on fair terms with everyone else in society is thus an unearned privilege that members of non-oppressed groups benefit from.

One example of this kind of relative advantage arises from women's risk of sexual violence in a culture where we face this danger at exponentially higher rates than men. This asymmetrical risk results in what the journalist and activist Susan Brownmiller terms a "male protection racket"—an informal social arrangement that lets all men benefit from the immoral actions of the specific few men who actually assault women.[3] Women's legitimate fear of sexual violence by men in general gives individual men the opportunity to benefit from being seen as Nice Guys who are willing to come to women's assistance. At their most innocuous, Nice Guys merely enjoy the warm and fuzzy psychological and social rewards bestowed on those deemed to be of upstanding character. At their worst, Nice Guys bemoan the injustice of being "friend-zoned" when their basic courtesies aren't rewarded with sex.*

---

* This isn't to suggest that all men who walk women to their cars late at night, or do whatever else they can to make women feel safe, are in some way intending to exploit or take advantage of women's vulnerability. Nor does it mean they should stop doing these things! It's just to point out that men's opportunity to perform these courtesies both results from and ultimately helps strengthen oppressive structures that systematically benefit them at women's expense.

Oppression isn't the sort of thing you experience as an individual in all your idiosyncratic glory. Instead, it's something that happens to you because of who society understands you to be, because of which boxes you've been sorted into. This is what feminists mean when they say women are oppressed *as women*—women are considered as deserving certain restrictive treatment because we're members of a particular social group. (So too when we say people of color are oppressed *as people of color.* Or that queer people are oppressed *as queer.*) This focus on social group membership also makes sense of the much-misunderstood feminist insistence that men can't be oppressed. When feminists make this statement they're not claiming that men can't be *harmed*—that would be absurd. Instead, when feminists say men can't be oppressed they're saying that men can't be harmed in a very specific way: men can't be oppressively harmed *as men.* They can't be oppressively harmed because of their gender. (Similarly, white people can't be oppressively harmed because of their race, and straight people can't be oppressively harmed because of their sexual orientation.) If I walk up to a guy and start kicking him in the shins, there's no question that I'm harming him, but the point here is that this harm would be random and unconnected to other related sorts of harms. There's no birdcage here, just a single wire. Even if the reason I'm kicking this guy is that I have a personal vendetta against men, and so there's a sense in which he *is* being harmed *as a man*, we don't live in a society where men in general face risks to their shins from marauding feminists.

In the all-things-considered balance, being a man benefits someone in our social world. This isn't to pretend that it's impossible for a man's gender to count against him. In some cases, for example, fathers lose custody disputes because they are men. It's fair to say that these men have been harmed because of their gender. But these harms don't count as oppressive because they stem from norms and institutions that, at the end of the day, work to men's advantage. A father who unfairly loses custody of his children because of a judge's unreflective belief that children belong with their mothers has still benefited, and will continue to benefit, from a lifetime of not being seen as the person primarily responsible for the care and feeding of the next generation of human beings. Even if a particular institution of patriarchy, such as the precedents of family law, systematically confers some benefits to women at the expense of men, on the whole this institution is part of a much larger network of formal and informal social norms and institutions—wires in a birdcage—that systematically benefit men, not women. Women's tendency to be awarded the custody of their children in these disputes can be traced, in large part, to the widely held sexist belief that women are more naturally suited to raise children than men. This belief, in conjunction with a host of other sexist beliefs about men's and women's natures, abilities, and appropriate social roles, combined with sexist social institutions that reflect and perpetuate these beliefs, on balance disadvantage women and benefit men.* So, while not being awarded the custody of their children is clearly a harm to some men, this harm isn't an oppressive one.

Let me beat this dead horse one last time because in my experience it tends to be a sticking point: *Oppression is a particular kind of harm or injustice.* Just because a harm or injustice isn't oppressive doesn't mean it isn't harmful or unjust. It just means it's a different kind of harm or injustice. A non-oppressive harm or injustice might even be much more severe than an oppressive

---

* And what's more, it's not clear whether being awarded the custody of their children always counts as an unambiguous benefit for women. After divorce, women's standard of living tends to decrease markedly while men's increases. This is due in part to the costs and lack of job flexibility associated with the responsibilities of raising children.

one—judgments of oppressiveness are a matter of a harm's or injustice's relationship to other harms and injustices, not a matter of their asperity. Oppressive harms and injustices are those that derive from social institutions that, *all things considered*, benefit members of one group at the expense of another. This means that you can't actually tell whether a harm or injustice is oppressive if you're looking at it in isolation. You need to look at the big picture to tell whether what you have on your hands is an isolated incident or a wire in a birdcage.

INDIVIDUAL PEOPLE VERSUS SYSTEMIC INSTITUTIONS

Another respect in which oppressive harms and injustices differ from your garden-variety harms and injustices has to do with their ability to transpire without any particular person actually intending them. According to the philosopher Iris Marion Young, oppression most often results from the "unconscious assumptions and reactions of well-meaning people in ordinary interactions, media and cultural stereotypes, and structural features of bureaucratic hierarchies and market mechanisms—in short, the normal processes of everyday life."[4] The occasional oppressive harm or injustice might result from a misogynist jerk having the conscious thought, "Ooh, look! A woman! Those bitches deserve mistreatment!" and acting accordingly, but this is the exception, not the rule. Far more often, you can't point to one individual person who's guilty of oppressing another.

Oppression isn't usually best understood as an individual moral wrong, but rather as a social or political wrong that arises through the unjust allocation of power or resources. It's often less about how individual people choose to interact with one another and more about how society is set up, about how our individual choices are structured by what's possible for us given the explicit rules and informal norms of our social world. It's far more often a matter of illegitimate imbalances of power than a matter of individual abuses of power per se. Philosopher Sally Haslanger makes sense of this point by making a distinction between *agent* oppression and *structural* oppression.[5]

Most manifestations of oppression are structural, not agential, Haslanger argues. When oppression is structural it's something that stems from our collective arrangements, from our background social hierarchies, from our unjust laws, institutions, or practices. Structural oppression can arise from explicit formal discrimination, such as the laws that enforced racial segregation in the Jim Crow South. It can arise from practices that are rooted not in animosity but mere thoughtlessness or indifference, such as the architectural practice of designing buildings with no access ramps for people who are disabled. It can arise from informal cultural norms and practices, such as those that disproportionately burden women with domestic and care work. What's important to notice is that each of these wires in the birdcage of structural oppression involve unfair dispensing of power, making it easier for members of a privileged social group to make their way in the world than members of a subordinated social group.

While structural oppression is sometimes caused intentionally—say, by racist or sexist policymakers looking to formally enshrine their worldview—far more often it results from a structure that exists without there being any particular agent who's responsible for it.* But we're not used to thinking about harms or injustices in this way. We tend to think that if some-

---

* This isn't to say that oppression is *never* agential. Sometimes it really does boil down to bad people doing bad things. Haslanger refuses to reduce oppression to structural explanations in all cases because that would make it impossible to distinguish people who abuse their social power to actively do things that are wrong from those who are members of privileged groups but try to avoid exploiting their unearned social power.

thing bad has happened then, unless it's an act of God, there must be someone we can point to who shoulders the blame, someone we can hold responsible. We like there to be a smoking gun. But oppressive harms and injustices don't usually work this way.

Most of the time, oppression's structures chug along in the background, subtly constraining what's possible for people without most of us even noticing what's going on. This means that oppression has a tendency to fly beneath our collective radar. Properly appreciating what this does to our ordinary ways of thinking about privilege and responsibility requires yet another metaphor: *the invisible knapsack*.

The Invisible Knapsack

The social groups we're sorted into usually aren't up to us. This makes for a sense in which it's not our fault when the world is just easier for us than it is for others. A person can't ask to be born white, male, rich, able-bodied, or cisgender, for example. While each of these unchosen aspects of their identity gives them a leg up in the world, it isn't necessarily clear what they could do to renounce these unearned privileges. You might think the unchosen nature of most of the social groups in question quashes any responsibility people might have for maintaining and benefiting from the birdcages of oppression.

Still, we *are* responsible for how we deal with our un-earned privileges. How we respond to the circumstances of oppression we find ourselves in—whether we indulge in our social group's comforts or resist them—is up to us. Even though it's inescapable that we operate within larger social structures, most of the time we can and should take responsibility for how we choose to act within these constrained sets of options. The appropriate response to the recognition that oppression's forces are often primarily structural isn't to throw our hands up and decide we're powerless to affect change so we might as well abandon the sisterhood and just try to get ours. We need to recognize and own up to our unearned privilege.

The structural nature of oppression means that it's possible for us to benefit from the oppression of others even if we aren't directly responsible for causing it. But recognizing that we might not deserve full credit for our successes in life can be hard to do. The comforting myth of meritocracy runs deep. No one's life is easy from the perspective of the person actually living it, after all. We alone know firsthand how hard we've worked, how much gratification we've deferred, how many challenges and setbacks and disappointments we've weathered. After all these long days and nights trapped in what author David Foster Wallace called our "skull-sized kingdoms," it's perhaps understandable that we like to think we're completely responsible for our achievements.[6] Even if we're good progressives, it's far easier to grant that other people are disadvantaged than it is to admit that we might be overprivileged, that we might not have earned fair and square everything that's come to us.

This point about the nature of privilege is driven home with a metaphor that was introduced by the feminist and anti-racist scholar Peggy McIntosh.[7] Discussing racism rather than sexism, McIntosh characterizes white privilege as "an invisible package of unearned assets that I can count on cashing in each day, but about which I was 'meant' to remain oblivious. White privilege is like an invisible weightless knapsack of special provisions, maps, passports, codebooks, visas, clothes, tools, and blank checks."[8] This invisible knapsack equips white people with the tools and advantages they need to thrive in a society structured by and for people like them. As a white person like McIntosh I can curse, or wear thrift-store clothing, or fail to answer an email, or talk with my mouth full, or run out to the store with smudged makeup and bedhead, or arrive late to a meeting, or get piercings and tattoos, or simply just have a bad day without having people chalk it up to the inferiority of my race. I can do well in a challenging situation without being called a credit to my race. I can easily buy "flesh-colored" bandages or crayons or dolls for my daughter that actually match our skin tone. I can get behind the wheel of my car and speed a bit without much worry about having the cops pulling me over for "driving while black." I can turn on the TV, surf the internet, or open a book or newspaper and see the perspectives of people of my race widely represented. I don't have to allocate extra time in my travel schedule to make it through airport security because of the greater chance of being picked out for a "random" search. I don't have to teach my daughter to be terrified of the police (although she already is, and I'll admit to not doing everything in my power to dissuade her of this fear).

"There are very few African American men in this country who haven't had the experience of being followed when they were shopping in a department store. That includes me," President Barack Obama told the nation in 2013, describing the paucity of the contents of his invisible knapsack in a speech after the neighborhood-watch vigilante George Zimmerman was acquitted for shooting and killing a black high school student named Trayvon Martin.[9] "There are very few African American men who haven't had the experience of walking across the street and hearing the locks click on the doors of cars. That happens to me, at least before I was a senator. There are very few African Americans who haven't had the experience of getting on an elevator to find a woman clutching her purse nervously and holding her breath until she had a chance to get off. That happens often." What does this do to a person? What does a lifetime of being treated with suspicion and distrust and low-level animosity do to your ability to engage with the people around you? I wouldn't know. As a white person, my invisible knapsack includes a magical potion that makes me appear innocent and harmless and trustworthy. I like to joke that I should bolster my professor salary with a side gig as a drug mule—nobody in their right mind, after all, would ever go rifling through a nice white lady's purse.

The people who are born into groups with more social privileges have the responsibility to create more fairness in society. This isn't the kind of responsibility that hinges straightforwardly on judgments about which people deserve what—neither in the sense of deserving punishment for doing something wrong, nor in the sense of deserving a reward for doing something right. This kind of responsibility means people being willing to rectify an imbalance caused by privileges that they'd never have had if our society were truly fair. At the very least, this responsibility requires a willingness to admit that there's a problem to be solved. And it requires that we reject the sentiment expressed so memorably by Voltaire's eternally optimistic Candide, that all we have to do is cultivate our own garden and expect the world to somehow take care of itself. Instead, socially privileged people need to take seriously the possibility that they should renounce some of the perks they never should have had to begin with.

Coming to understand these dynamics of oppression involves threading a tricky needle. We need to recognize that our social world is comprised of structures that existed long before we came along and that these structures constrain what's possible for all of us. But we also need to recognize that we're usually capable of acting with some degree of responsibility within these structures; we need an honest reckoning about what we can and can't control. Feminist analyses of oppression, then, always aim to strike a balance between agential and structural explanations of our social world. The birdcage metaphor shows that the proper level of analysis for feminism isn't really at the level of what an individual woman does or doesn't do in a sexist society. Feminists are after the big picture. We're less interested in passing judgment on how individual women choose to navigate their birdcages than in trying to get people to pay attention to all the damned wires.

All of us are guilty of complicity in our social systems, to one degree or another. We're social animals, inescapably influenced by the norms and expectations of the world around us. None of us escapes without drinking at least a little of the Kool-Aid. We, even those who are oppressed, can't help but take in what our social world instills in us about what we're supposed to be like, what we're supposed to desire. Oppression isn't just imposed upon us from without. It's also something we internalize.

The Panopticon

Another metaphor that's useful for understanding the distinctive dynamics of oppression comes from the French philosopher and historian Michel Foucault. He was fascinated by the Panopticon, an eighteenth-century prison model invented by the English philosopher and social theorist Jeremy Bentham. The Panopticon works by having a single guard in a central tower watch over the many prisoners whose cells circle the tower in a ring. Because they never know if or when they're actually being watched by the guard, prisoners in a Panopticon become their own jailers—in effect, disciplining and punishing themselves. Foucault argues that modern society functions similarly: we come to think of ourselves as permanently visible and we start policing our behavior, perpetually surveilling ourselves and docilely falling in line with the status quo. In such a world, speculates Foucault, "there is no need for arms, physical violence, material constraints. Just a gaze. An inspecting gaze, a gaze which each individual under its weight will end by interiorising to the point that he is his own overseer, each individual thus exercising this surveillance over, and against himself."[10] Modern power made its mark on the world, Foucault argues, by inventing new forms of social control that outsource the pesky work of making people do things they don't want to do onto—or, more accurately, *into*—the people themselves. No need for tyrants or coercive police states when the subjects can be convinced it was their own idea to fall in line.

Oppression is almost never the result of plans hatched up by an Orwellian cabal of men with nuclear codes who're plotting how to keep women in their place so men can make their golf tee-times and reap all the other benefits of the heteropatriarchy. We're not talking *Animal Farm* or *Brave New World* or *Dr. Strangelove* here. But occasionally it can be instructive if we pretend that we are. Imagine, for a moment, that you're in charge of controlling massive numbers of people. What's the best way to get them to do what you want? What would the most effective method of social control look like? Surely not a soldier on every corner—too expensive, unwieldy, unpredictable, inefficient. (Not to mention kind of vulgar and tacky.) Far more elegant to get people to do the work for you. What's needed is surveillance. Constant surveillance. When it's best to assume that you're always being watched, you tend to make sure that you're not doing anything unsanctioned.*

We don't have to be forced to do something if we can be convinced that it was our idea to do it, when we experience the relevant motivation as an internal desire rather than an external influence. This concept is as plain as day to anyone who's ever resorted to reverse psychology when parenting a recalcitrant

---

* It's worth marveling at Foucault's prescience in coming up with this stuff in the 1970s, well before the invention of current-day technology like facial-recognition software, social media check-ins, cell-phone GPS tracking, and everything else that's virtually guaranteed the death of privacy.

toddler: "Don't put your shoes on, kiddo! Whatever you do, keep those shoes off!" can be the most effective way to get a kid who's determined to exercise her own will out the door in the morning. As we get older it's usually a little more difficult to pull the wool over our eyes, so the methods of manipulation need to get more sophisticated. But the basic principle remains the same: people can be recruited to act as their own jailers.

FEMINIST APPLICATIONS OF THE PANOPTICON

Feminist philosophers such as Sandra Bartky extend Foucault's Panopticon metaphor to analyze the ways that women, in particular, end up policing their bodies, minds, emotions, and behaviors to fit the expectations of conventional femininity. Foucault tends to talk about the way power functions in modernity in terms of "disciplinary practices" that produce what he calls "docile bodies." (So, for example, factory workers must clock in and out at precisely prescribed times, soldiers must line up in straight rows, schoolchildren must sit motionless at their desks.) Bartky points out that we live in a world that requires women's bodies to be significantly more disciplined and docile than men's. This discipline and docility take several different forms: the feminine body is required to be a specific shape and size, it's required to move in precisely the right ways, and it's required to be displayed as an ornamented surface. "The woman who checks her makeup half a dozen times a day to see if her foundation has caked or her mascara run, who worries that the wind or rain may spoil her hairdo, who looks frequently to see if her stockings have bagged at the ankle, or who, feeling fat, monitors everything she eats," Bartky argues, "has become, just as surely as an inmate of the Panopticon, a self-policing subject, a self committed to a relentless self-surveillance. This self-surveillance is a form of obedience to patriarchy."[11]

To be clear, this isn't merely to rehash the now-familiar feminist grievance about how unrealistic and unfair beauty standards are for women in a world where Instagram filters and cosmetic surgery and Photoshop fixes are ubiquitous. The point here is about thought and behavior: when these gendered standards are internalized, they function as an insidious form of *social control*. Women's bodies are controlled in order to ultimately control their minds. "Standards of beauty describe in precise terms the relationship that an individual will have to her own body," writes Andrea Dworkin. "They prescribe her motility, spontaneity, posture, gait, the uses to which she can put her body. They define precisely the dimensions of her physical freedom. And of course, the relationship between physical freedom and psychological development, intellectual possibility, and creative potential is an umbilical one."[12]

What happens to the mind when the body is systematically constrained? It's not a comforting thought, but are any of us really going to pretend that caged birds sing as often or as well as those who are free? Even if the birdcage of femininity is gilded, it's still a cage.

Feminists have been giving us versions of this criticism for a very long time. As Mary Wollstonecraft bemoaned all the way back in 1792,

> To preserve personal beauty, woman's glory! the limbs and faculties are cramped with worse than Chinese bands, and the sedentary life which they are condemned to live, whilst boys frolic in the open air, weakens the muscles and relaxes the nerves.... Genteel women are, literally speaking, slaves to their bodies, and glory in their subjection.... Taught from their infancy that beauty is woman's sceptre, the mind shapes itself to the body and, roaming round its gilt cage, only seeks to adorn its prison.[13]

Let these words sink in: *the mind shapes itself to the body*. The concern here isn't just that the beauty and frivolity and femininity required of girls and women is a waste of time, or that it's not as lofty as the pursuits open to boys and men. The worry is that what's permissible or required for girls and women to do with and to their bodies determines what's possible for them to do with their minds. When a little girl is told to stop wiggling and "sit like a lady" it's not just her body she's being taught to rein in. When she's fussed over and told to be careful in even slightly precarious situations it's not just her body she's being taught is untrustworthy. When grown women then fail to reach the heights of success or genius found in men, this is in part attributable to a lifetime of being made to know that we're fundamentally incapable.

Iris Marion Young explores the mutually reinforcing interrelationship between body and mind in her influential analysis of empirical studies that look at gendered differences in how girls and boys throw a ball.[14] Young found these studies confirming a familiar stereotype, one where boys tend to use more physical space and energy while girls tend to shrink and deform their physical gestures. Picture the two throwing styles in your mind. There's a reason "throwing like a girl" is an insult: it's a crappy and inept way to throw a ball. But there's no reason to think this ineptitude has anything to do with the physical differences between boys and girls, Young insists. Particularly when they're prepubescent, the differences between girls' and boys' bodies are quite small— certainly not significant enough to explain the vast differences in their stereotypical throwing styles. Instead, she speculates that these differences result from a particular self-fulfilling prophecy. Girls (and women) are taught to see their bodies as fragile and burdensome, as things to be "looked at and acted upon" rather than used or harnessed to effectively navigate the world.[15] We're taught to be afraid of taking up too much space and to be afraid of getting hurt. When these beliefs about what we're capable of are internalized they become our reality. "We decide beforehand—usually mistakenly—that the task is beyond us, and thus give it less than our full effort."[16] So we throw like girls.

And instead of trying to see what we can do with these incompetent bodies of ours, we content ourselves with obsessing over what they look like.

INTERNALIZED OBJECTIFICATION

More than 100 years ago, the sociologist and activist W. E. B. Du Bois coined the term *double consciousness* to explain how black people must learn to experience the world through two different sets of eyes, seeing themselves as they're seen by white people as well as on their own terms. "It is a peculiar sensation . . . this sense of always looking at one's self through the eyes of others, of measuring one's soul by the tape of a world that looks on in amused contempt and pity," he laments.[17] Feminists argue that women have to live with a similar kind of double vision, learning to see ourselves first and foremost as we appear to men who appreciate us primarily for our sexual attractiveness. "In contemporary patriarchal culture," Bartky writes, "a panoptical male connoisseur resides within the consciousness of most women: They stand perpetually before his gaze and under his judgement. Woman lives her body as seen by another, by an anonymous patriarchal Other."[18] In the wake of the work of the film theorist Laura Mulvey, feminists refer to this phenomenon as the internalization of the *male gaze*.[19] Mulvey argues that because our visual culture is made principally by men and for men, it depicts the world in general, and women in particular, from men's point of view. It portrays women as existing primarily for the sexual appreciation and pleasure of men—as sex objects.

This message is ubiquitous, and women internalize it. "Women live in objectification the way fish live in water," Catharine Mac-Kinnon reminds us.[20] We're surrounded by it, but we also come to need it, and some days, even like it. We end up in the weird position of actually longing for and seeking out something we know (or should know) is bad for us. We know it's insulting to be treated like a piece of meat, as existing chiefly for men's sexual amusement, but we simultaneously feel bad when we're not treated this way. Given how often women receive the subtle (and not-so-subtle) message that our worth is determined by whether we're sexually pleasing to men, it's probably not surprising that we find ourselves in this position.

It's no wonder, really, that women internalize the male gaze. Think about how early the indoctrination starts. We incessantly tell infant girls that they're pretty instead of telling them that they're smart or strong or tough or funny. *Pretty, pretty, pretty, pretty, pretty.* We dress them in scratchy lace and slap absurd pink bows on their bald heads. We surround our preschoolers with princess paraphernalia and encourage them to fantasize about being rescued by Prince Charming. Spend eight seconds in a toy store and you'll know all you need to know about how ubiquitous this cultural training is: aisle after pink aisle of sexed-up Barbie dolls, play makeup, even tiny little high heels to play dress-up in. "Tippy shoes," my daughter called them at four when she was begging for a pair. I mean, if she stands a snowball's chance in hell of actually being able to walk in them better than her pathetically clumsy mother, I probably should've started her then. But I refused to do the patriarchy's work of inculcating her with the belief that she's exactly as valuable as she is sexy, that her worth is determined by whether she's aesthetically pleasing to dudes. It's not like I could entirely prevent it—the Disney princess juggernaut cannot be stopped—but at least I wanted to go down fighting. So no tippy shoes. And no calling her "pretty." I banned the word from the household. Turns out that, when push comes to shove, people can usually come up with other adjectives to tell you how cute your kid is.

Still, lest you think I fancy myself above all this cultural brainwashing, let me make it clear that I'm writing this with my stomach rumbling from having skipped lunch, the underwire from my bra digging into my rib cage, and mascara flaking into my eyes. It's obvious that social forces influence the desires we come to have. Anyone who's suffered the self-imposed indignity of enduring an evening wearing an excruciatingly uncomfortable but unbelievably stylish pair of shoes can attest to this conundrum. Social forces can make us want things that we almost certainly wouldn't want in the absence of these forces. This kind of influence might not strike us as a particularly bad thing; we are, after all, social creatures, so we should expect a great deal of who we are and what we want to be shaped by the society we live in. But the real problem is that social forces are capable of making us desire things that are patently not in our best interest, or fail to desire things that are.

BADLY ADAPTIVE PREFERENCES

Philosophers call this the problem of *badly adaptive preferences*. Impractical shoes are one thing; choices that threaten your actual well-being are quite another. These choices can range from dangerous and unnecessary plastic surgeries to eating disorders to buying into the cultural valorization of feminine self-sacrifice that expects a good wife and mother to put the needs of her family before her own. The canonical example of badly adaptive preferences comes from Aesop's fable of the fox and the grapes.[21] Just as when the fox realizes that he can't get the grapes he wants and so decides that they're probably sour, people can respond to the recognition that many worthwhile things are outside their grasp by rejecting the value of these things and deciding not to pursue them. The issue here is that those grapes are just fine, and the fox has every reason to want them. He's being irrational when he pretends that they're sour. So too, you might think, are women who starve or mutilate or even just inconvenience themselves in our quixotic attempts to approximate the impossible ideals of femininity.

Badly adaptive preferences present a problem for your "live free or die" types who think we shouldn't be in the business of evaluating people's desires, that grown adults should instead be left alone to do whatever they want no matter how manifestly ill-advised.* But if the unjust social circumstances of oppression can make people prefer things that are bad for them, or fail to prefer things that are good for them, then we're not going to get to the root of this injustice unless we're allowed to have *something* to say about the content of people's desires.

So what are we supposed to think when women willingly take on the work of disciplining and punishing themselves? Should we think of it as a situation where we're being coerced into doing things against our will—where we're hapless victims of the patriarchy left with no choice but to conform to beauty standards that are imposed upon us externally, despite what we ourselves might want? If the alternative is to think, as philosopher Susan Bordo puts it, that it's "in our essential feminine nature to be (delightfully if incomprehensibly) drawn to such trivialities, and to be willing to endure whatever physical inconvenience is required, . . . [that] we 'do it to ourselves' [and] are our 'own worst enemies,'" then the women-as-victims explanation has its appeal.[22] Understanding women's obedience to patriarchal beauty standards as bond-

---

* History is full of misguided attempts to force people to do things for their own good, after all, so the general antifascist consensus these days is that we're better off letting people make their own mistakes than we are assuming we know what's best for them.

age rather than choice makes sense of the intuition that there's something wrong with the world, not with us.

But let's be real: we're not blowing our paychecks at Sephora and shooting our faces full of Botox because there's a gun to our head. And men aren't the only enemy here—at least, not all men. This explanation, one that paints men as the all-powerful oppressors and women as the powerless oppressed, leaves us with no way to make sense of the men who are just going along with a system they didn't create, don't control, and don't necessarily even agree with. And what's worse, it fails to acknowledge the extent to which women collude with sexism—including, for example, our often extremely enthusiastic participation in the very practices that objectify and oppress us, and when we impose these practices on other women and on our daughters.

I'm quite certain that I'm not alone in feeling naked if I go out in public without wearing makeup. I know I'm not the only femme with a closet full of agonizing shoes she hardly ever wears. I'll confess to spending a truly shocking percentage of my monthly budget on waxing, haircuts, and mani/pedis. No one is forcing me to do any of this stuff, and I'd be lying if I pretended that I didn't enjoy it. How, then, are to we to understand my responsibility here? "Within a Foucauldian framework," writes Bordo,

> power and pleasure do not cancel each other. Thus, the heady experience of feeling powerful, or "in control," far from being a necessarily accurate reflection of one's actual social position, is always suspect as itself the product of power relations whose shape may be very different. Within such a framework, too, one can acknowledge that women are not always passive "victims" of sexism, but that we may contribute to the perpetuation of female subordination ... without this entailing that we have "power" (or are equally positioned with men) in sexist culture.[23]

Bordo's point here, in part, is that making sense of oppression requires going back and forth between agential and structural explanations, and that if we insist on conceptualizing things only in terms of one or the other we'll fail to grasp the entire picture. When women manage to feel some sense of pleasure or ownership or competence when we participate in a sexist system that serves us up as treats for men, this doesn't mean the system is off the hook, nor does it erase the power differences that constrain our choices within it. But it also doesn't necessarily make us dupes who have no idea what we're doing.

How should we, with our feminist hats on, respond to the suspicion (or straight-up recognition) that a woman's preferences have been shaped by internalized oppression? There's a temptation to get judgey here, and I'm not going to pretend that feminists (present authorial company included) have never criticized those women whose choices endorse sexism in particularly egregious ways. (Bertrand Russell once quipped that the bulk of morality is just the cruel satisfaction of judging others.)[24] I'm not proud of it, but I'll fess up to a few snarky comments about a friend's new girlfriend's breast implants. Many of my feminist friends were willing to give my condescension a pass, but a transman friend was not. If you're trans you get that you don't question or judge other people's decisions to do what they want to their bodies in order to fulfill their desired gender expression. You get that we're all just trying to get by in a world not of our choosing. You get that it might be easier or more satisfying to go after individual people than it is to take on the amorphous system that impels our choices, but that the victories of the former are almost always pyrrhic. You get that there's no point in judging or shaming people for doing what they need to do to survive.

My friend's open-mindedness is instructive: when we focus too single-mindedly on how individual women choose to navigate their birdcage we have a tendency to lose sight of the wires.

At the end of the day, what we really want is a revolution, and no revolution was ever brought about by punching down.

A COLLECTIVE ACTION PROBLEM

Philosopher Ann Cudd identifies a collective action problem here, where it can often make sense for women to comply with the demands of a sexist society because the short-term benefits of cooperation outweigh the long-shot possibilities of ushering in a new world order.* In such cases, Cudd argues, women "are co-opted through their own short-run rational choices to reinforce the long-run oppression of their social group."[25] Think about all the concrete things a woman stands to gain by acquiescing, and think about what she has to lose. There's the economic advantage (or necessity) of finding a man willing to financially support you and your children in a world with a wage gap and the expectation that you'll take on most of the uncompensated work required to raise kids and run a household. (High-minded political ideals are great and all, but you've still gotta eat.) There's the need to find a man to protect you in a sexually violent culture that targets women.† (Identifying a "male protection racket," Susan Brownmiller argues that rape ensures women's continued dependence on men by making male protection necessary.)[26] And then there are the more amorphous perks. There are significant psychological benefits attached to social approval, of feeling like those around you understand and accept and affirm how you choose to live your life. (We're social animals, built to seek

---

* A collective action problem is a scenario where the end result would be better for everyone involved if everyone cooperates with one another, but they fail to do so because each person is slightly better off if they don't cooperate. This way of thinking about the difficulties of joint action has been a staple of political philosophy and game theory for centuries.
† More on this in Chapter 5.

the approval of those with whom we identify.) There's the chance you might be able to avoid the burnout that comes from being hyperattuned to every injustice in the world. (Being mad about everything all the time is emotionally exhausting.) There's the prospect of erotic gratification in a culture where you've been socialized by what Bartky calls the "mechanisms of desire" to find male dominance sexually exciting.[27] (It turns out people can be motivated to do much of the work of oppressing themselves if it's tied to their sexual desires, those deepest and most opaque parts of their psyches.)*

OK, so there are perks to going with the flow. Add in the depressing odds of large-scale social change happening in any of our lifetimes, and the decision to just get yours starts to seem awfully reasonable.

Every one of us finds ourselves navigating a social world that presents a limited number of options of what choices, behaviors, and life projects are acceptable for people like us, and a limited number of resources over which we're usually competing with others. We aren't deluded when we knuckle to. Women are often making rational, clear-eyed calculations of what our best odds are for living a decent life, given the competition for scarce resources. We should think of women as "bargaining with patriarchy," as Uma Narayan puts it.† Narayan counsels us to be aware not just of how an oppressive society imposes constraints

---

* More on this in Chapter 6.
† Narayan makes this claim in the context of criticizing Western feminists' tendency to portray non-Western women as if their agency were completely "pulverized" by patriarchy, arguing that this undermines the value and significance of the choices these women make "from the point of view of the women who make them." While not her intent, Narayan's insight can be extended to analyzing the lives of Western women as well.

on women's choices but also how women are capable of making choices within these constraints.[28]

But the problem is that the decisions women make to take care of ourselves far too often have the result—intended or not—of screwing over other women. When a middle-class white woman leans in to her career and doesn't have a husband willing to lean out, it's almost always an underpaid and exploited woman of color who fills in the gaps. When a woman capable of approximating traditional beauty ideals invests in her femininity to catch a man (or even just because it's good for the ego to be flattered by male attention), she makes things worse for women who can't or won't be seen as conventionally attractive. When a woman with kids takes the inevitable hit to her career so she can take care of her family, she implicitly affirms a world in which women and not men are expected to make these sacrifices. When a straight woman indulges the misogynistic pornographic fantasies of her male partner because she wants to please her man (or even because she herself has eroticized these scripts), she helps maintain a sexual culture that eroticizes gendered relationships of dominance and submission. When a woman in the middle of a contentious divorce takes advantage of the judge's unreflective preference in favor of granting custody to mothers to get custody of her kids, she helps shore up the idea that women and not men are primarily responsible for raising children.* When a woman turns a blind eye to the well-founded rumors that her boss enjoys his interns maybe a little too much

---

* This particular bugaboo is a favorite of men's right's activists, who seem to think that this one injustice faced by men in the battle of the sexes is enough to balance the scales against all other injustices faced by women. MRAs also seem not to realize that most feminists—who, again, are not generally in the habit of unthinkingly affirming every choice a woman makes—are even more critical of the social norms that underlie this phenomenon than they are.

because he's never gone after her personally and she's up for a promotion, she helps ensure that the workplace will remain a hostile environment for too many. And on it goes.

These collective action problems help explain the resiliency of the patriarchy. Women often have very good reason to go along with things, even though doing so makes it worse for them, and all other women, in the long run.

Cages made up of seemingly insignificant wires, backpacks full of invisible provisions, prisons that use mind control to get you to do the dirty work for them—as you can see, sexist oppression is nothing if not creative in its methods. But the thing is, sexism isn't the only form of oppression lurking in the shadows. Gender isn't the only, nor even always the most significant, social grouping that determines people's life prospects. Making sense of how significantly more complicated oppression can be requires yet another metaphor.

The Traffic Intersection

"Consider an analogy to traffic in an intersection, coming and going in all four directions. Discrimination, like traffic through an intersection, may flow in one direction, and it may flow in another. If an accident happens in an intersection, it can be caused by cars traveling from any number of directions and, sometimes, from all of them."[29] Critical race theorist and legal activist Kimberlé Crenshaw uses the experience of standing at a corner of a busy intersection to describe the experience of living through overlapping oppressions, concretizing an idea and coining a term for a phenomenon other black feminists like Anna Julia Cooper had started talking about over a century earlier: *intersectionality*. Just as multiple intersecting lanes of traffic multiply your risk of getting into an accident, multiple intersecting oppressions multiply your risk of experiencing injustice. And just as the risks of getting into an accident can't be measured or anticipated beforehand nor the causes of an accident understood after the fact if we only ever examine each lane of traffic individually, the nature of multiple oppressive injustices isn't something you can make sense of by trying to look at their sources separately. Intersectionality illustrates how people who occupy multiple marginalized social positions experience oppression that is qualitatively and quantitatively different from those with fewer social disadvantages.

When describing the injustices faced by someone who's multiply oppressed, it's not like you can step back and carve up their list of grievances like "This awful thing happened to me because I'm a woman. But this *other* awful thing happened because I'm black. And this *third* awful thing happened because I'm poor, and this *fourth* awful thing is because I'm a lesbian." What this means, in the language of intersectionality, is that multiple oppressions aren't additive, they're *multiplicative*. So, for example, we shouldn't think of the oppression that a black woman experiences as being because of "race + gender" but as being because of "racialized gender." The crucial insight of intersectionality is that the oppression experienced by a black woman doesn't exist in the overlapping area in a Venn diagram comprised of all the bad things that white women experience and all the bad things that black men experience. Instead, it is its own entirely unique experience.

Intersectional theorists focus on how social categories such as race, class, gender, ability, et cetera, react through their relationships with one another. They argue that because the model we're using here is multiplicative, not additive, we shouldn't think of these categories as layering on top of one another but as mixing together in complex and sometimes unpredictable ways.

Intersectionality is especially useful in making sense of how personal identity functions in oppressive contexts. There are several other useful metaphors philosophers have come up with to illustrate intersectionalist insights about identity. Philosopher Elizabeth Spelman puts things in terms of those pop-bead toys you might've made necklaces out of when you were a kid.[30] We shouldn't think of identity as being like pop beads, Spelman posits, where who you are is determined by identity categories that can be snapped together or apart at will. In this mistaken view—which Spelman also amusingly refers to as "tootsie roll metaphysics"—each gender bead, race bead, and class bead is in principle separable from the others; the experience of each is identical for everyone within that identity category; and the significance of each is uninfluenced by the others. "On this view of personal identity . . . my being a woman means the same whether I am white or Black, rich or poor, French or Jamaican, Jewish or Muslim."[31] But this is manifestly false. What it's like to be a woman is fundamentally different depending on what the rest of your life looks like. Your hopes and dreams, your guiding values, your relationships with others, your sense of what's appropriate or desirable or even possible for someone like you—each of these and more is informed by a byzantine interplay of where your identity fits in terms of race, class, sexuality, and so on. Pretending that there's some essential core of femininity shared in common across these lines, as we'll see, is a recipe for disaster.

Speaking of recipes, the Latin American philosopher María Lugones goes a different route in her exploration of multiple oppressions, analyzing intersectionality with a cooking metaphor.[32] Just as you can't entirely separate out the egg yolk, lemon juice, or oil after things go south when you're making mayonnaise and the ingredients curdle on you, Lugones says we should think of the identities of people who occupy multiple oppressed groups as made up of messy, intermeshed categories that can't be distilled into pure, separable parts. When an emulsion like mayonnaise curdles, the ingredients that had at one point been separate (yolk, lemon, oil) break up into something new (yolky oil or oily yolk), something different from and not reducible to the original ingredients. But while curdling is typically a bad thing in the kitchen, Lugones thinks it can be a good thing out in the world. The metaphor of curdling, for Lugones, serves as a call for people who are members of multiple oppressed groups to stop trying to fit into social categories, or live up to social expectations, that weren't made by or for people like them. Instead, Lugones advocates that multiply oppressed people—she focuses in particular on those who are "mestizaje," a mix of Spanish and Indigenous American heritages—embrace ambiguity and plurality when they define and live out their identities. "I think of something in the middle of either/or, something impure, something or someone mestizo, as both separated, curdled, and resisting in its curdled state."[33]

Lugones demonstrates what she has in mind for mestiza resistance in the format of the book in which she introduces these ideas, refusing to conform to the genre conventions of the academic monograph. Instead, she switches back and forth between English and Spanish, argument and autobiography, poetry and prose. This practice of resistance should be thought of as festive and cultivated as an art, she says, and it can take many forms, including

Bi- and multilingual experimentation;
code-switching;
categorial blurring and confusion;
caricaturing the selves we are in the worlds of our
    oppressors, infusing them with ambiguity;
practicing trickstery and foolery;
elaborate and explicitly marked gender transgression.[34]

We'll return to the insight that messing with conventions can be a way of sticking it to the Man when we look at philosopher Judith Butler's analysis of drag queens and kings in her influential critique of the ideology of gender. For now, the take-home message is that the more oppressed social groups you're a member of, the more you should anticipate experiences like not fitting into conventional expectations, like feeling not quite this but not quite that, like not seeing yourself represented in mainstream culture. But rather than experiencing this marginality as a sort of misfittedness or homelessness, and rather than trying to make yourself conform, Lugones asks you to embrace your transgressiveness as a condemnation of an overly constrained and unimaginative status quo. You're not the problem here; the world is.

THE BASEMENT

As a theoretical tool, intersectionality has been incredibly useful for documenting and explaining the distinctive harms and injustices experienced by those who are multiply oppressed. But an even more important upshot of intersectional analyses has been the overdue reckoning they've occasioned within the feminist movement. When taken to its logical conclusion, intersectionality lays bare the uncomfortable truth that the enemy doesn't always reside outside the feminist gates.

As we've seen, the patterned nature of oppressive advantages and disadvantages means the direction of oppressive forces runs from oppressor groups to oppressed groups. But it's important to remember that people can be, and often are, simultaneously members of both kinds of groups: you can be oppressed in virtue of some aspects of your identity and an oppressor in virtue of others. This means that oppression continues to function within liberation movements themselves. And it means that it's incredibly important that members of

such movements be willing to consider their roles in oppressing others.

This dynamic of intersectionality is captured in another
metaphor Crenshaw introduced: *a basement*. She saw that
intersectional oppression can work like being in a basement,
where people who are disadvantaged on the basis of one or a
few identities stand on the shoulders of those who are disadvantaged by a larger number of identities. Rather than focusing
on those who need help the most, anti-oppressive movements
have historically tended to concentrate on getting people who
are closest to the basement's escape hatch out, ignoring those
who are worse off. This hatch door acts as a sort of single-issue
filter. As long as you have only one issue holding you back, you
can get through the hatch on what Crenshaw calls the "but for"
rule: "those above the ceiling admit from the basement only
those who can say that 'but for' the ceiling, they too would be
in the upper room."[35] The only people getting out of the basement, in other words, are those who are barely trapped in it. In
feminist circles, that's women who are white, straight, cis, able-
bodied, and wealthy or middle-class. Not surprisingly, these
are the women who've been steering the ship in the feminist
movement.

The poster child for this blinkered form of feminist activism is probably Betty Friedan. In her bestselling 1963 book *The
Feminine Mystique,* Friedan helped put second-wave feminism
on the map in postwar America with her "problem that has no
name." The most disastrous problem a woman could possibly
face, as Friedan would have it, was the widespread dissatisfaction of those who lived in material comfort but failed to find their
lives as wives and mothers as fulfilling as prevailing cultural
narratives told them they were supposed to be. Friedan didn't
stop to consider the possibility that there might be worse fates
for a woman than the ennui shared by bored and understimu-

lated leisure-class housewives. Nor did she apparently care that her solution for this ennui—that white women be given access to the career opportunities enjoyed by white men—mostly outsourced the unrewarding domestic work these women were so anxious to escape to poor women of color.

"What woman...is so enamoured of her own oppression that she cannot see her heelprint upon another woman's face," asks Audre Lorde.[36] Friedan's mistake, bell hooks compellingly argues, was pretending that white women's experiences of oppression are even close to as bad as it can get.

> [*The Feminine Mystique*] remains a useful discussion of the impact of sexist discrimination on a select group of women. Examined from a different perspective, however, it can also be seen as a case study of narcissism, insensitivity, sentimentality, and self-indulgence, which reaches its peak when Friedan...makes a comparison between the psychological effects of isolation on white housewives and the impact of confinement on the self-concept of prisoners in Nazi concentration camps.[37]

Friedan's dubious application of the "but for" rule wasn't limited to women of color. Despite being a founder and the first president of the National Organization of Women (NOW), she tried to keep lesbians out of the feminist movement, painting them as a "lavender menace" whose inclusion risked derailing feminist gains by playing into the negative stereotypes held by feminism's critics.

hooks argues that Friedan's shortsightedness is typical of white feminism in general, which has tended to universalize a particular experience of relative privilege (characterized by the absence of racist, heterosexist, classist, and ableist oppression) as "the" experience of women in general. Feminism's pretense that there's an essential core of femininity shared by all women has, again and again throughout the movement's history, ended up falsely enshrining the experiences of the most privileged women as the experiences of all women. When you claim that everyone in the basement has it the same, you can ignore the fact that those who are closest to escaping it often have their feet on the faces of those below them.

Intersectionality corrects these tendencies, making sure that we pay attention to the way sexism affects all women, not just those who have the social capital to have their complaints about it heard or taken seriously. As we'll see in much more depressing detail, the feminist movement has too often tended to take two steps forward and one step back in regard to this insight, but I don't believe I'm being overly Pollyannaish by insisting that feminism is making some progress.

For example, the queer black feminist scholar Moya Bailey has recently given the racialized gender oppression experienced by black women a powerful new name: *misogynoir*. A portmanteau of "misogyny" and "noir" (the French word for "black") coined just a few years ago, misogynoir describes the racialized sexism that black women experience in a world that loathes them for both their race and their gender.[38] Being depicted in almost all hip-hop lyrics as being good for exactly two things—sex or abuse—is misogynoir. Being stereotyped as strong enough to endure physical or mental trauma that would level anyone else—whether it's caregiving for a white family's children or elderly for over twelve hours a day and seeing their own for just a few while earning less than minimum wage, or leaving children in a relative's care for a job in another country so they can provide better opportunities for their children, or having to step up as head of household when all the men in their community have been consumed by the prison-industrial complex, or being expected to keep quiet about sexual abuse lest they be seen as selling out their brothers—is misogynoir.[39] Receiving inadequate medical care or dying in childbirth at much greater rates than white women because physicians don't include black women in clinical trials or take their asserted physical concerns seriously is misogynoir.[40] These experiences of sexist oppression are unique to black women, and they're invisible to feminism as long as we insist on thinking of white womanhood as the textbook case.

Focusing in large part on how black women are portrayed in hip-hop lyrics and popular culture more generally, Bailey's term gave a name to a phenomenon that black feminists had been talking about for decades. Discussing the arrests, trial, and obscenity charges against the members of the rap group 2 Live Crew in the 1990s, for example, Crenshaw admitted,

> My immediate response . . . was ambivalence. I wanted to stand together with the brothers against a racist attack, but I wanted to stand *against* a frightening explosion of violent imagery directed at women like me. My sharp internal division—my dissatisfaction with the idea that the "real issue" is race or that the "real issue" is gender—is characteristic of my experience as a Black woman living at the intersection of racial and sexual subordination.[41]

The thought that black women occupy a social position that makes them especially well situated to tell us something important about how interlocking systems of oppression function in our world is echoed by other black feminists. The activist Frances Beale argued in 1970 that women of color are doubly oppressed in ways that white women rarely understand.[42] The sociologist Patricia Hill Collins confirmed this in her 1990 book, *Black Feminist Thought: Knowledge, Consciousness, and the Politics of Empowerment*, arguing that black women's particular histories at the intersection of multiple systems of power give them unique insight into how oppression functions in general.[43] Author and poet Alice Walker affirmed this by articulating a new social theory, *womanism*, that centers the history and experiences of women of color. "Womanist is to feminist as purple is to lavender," Walker explained, suggesting that womanism is a broader category than feminism; its focus encompasses not only gender inequalities but also the interlocking oppressions of race, class, and even nature.[44]

The importance of protecting and celebrating black women's voices was given perhaps its most powerful expression by Audre Lorde, who argues that when white feminists refuse to pay attention to the differences in women's lives they merely entrench existing systems of oppression. Aligning white feminists who don't see race as a feminist issue with white male slave-masters, Lorde explains that

> those of us who stand outside the circle of this society's definition of acceptable women; those of us who have been forged in the crucibles of difference—those of us who are poor, who are lesbians, who are Black, who are older—know that survival is not an academic skill. It is learning how to take our differences and make them strengths. For the master's tools will never dismantle the master's house. They may allow us temporarily to beat him at his own game, but they will never enable us to bring about genuine change. And this fact is only threatening to those women who still define the master's house as their only source of support.[45]

Lorde's influential claim that "the master's tools will never dismantle the master's house" has gone on to inspire a generation of feminist theorists to imagine new ways out of the patriarchal mess we're in.

CHAPTER 3

THE SOCIAL CONSTRUCTION OF GENDER

You know those goofy parties pregnant couples have where they invite their friends and family over and serve them cupcakes with blue or pink icing hidden in the middle to announce whether they're having a boy or a girl? Gender reveal parties, right?

Wrong. They're *sex* reveal parties. Sex is a biological concept; it has to do with what chromosomes or genitalia you have.* Gender, on the other hand, is a psychological and social concept; it

---

* Genitals are often taken to be equivalent to biological sex, but the issue is more complicated. Chromosomes and genitals don't always match up. And what people mean by "sex" often changes meaning for the purpose of excluding people. Clearly "sex" isn't picking out chromosomes at gender reveal parties because most people don't know what the kid's chromosomal profile actually is at that point. (The exceptions are those who opt for increasingly common procedures such as preimplantation genetic diagnosis prior to IVF, noninvasive prenatal testing, or amniocentesis, all of which provide parents with some information about the "genetic profile" of their impending child.) But when people want to exclude trans or intersex women from competing in athletic competitions, for example, they'll say that "sex" really picks out chromosomes or hormone levels, even if the athlete in question has female genitals. See Rachel McKinnon, "Participation in Sport Is a Human Right, Even for Trans Women," *APA Newsletter on LGBTQ Issues in Philosophy* 19, no. 1 (2019): 10–14.

has to do with the cultural and behavioral norms, roles, and expectations you identify with (and how others treat you in virtue of this identification). Last I checked, the only thing we're getting from ultrasounds is crotch shots. But much to the consternation of feminists and other gender theorists, people have started using the word "gender" as if it's just the word for sex you use in polite company—because the word "sex" also means something else entirely, and Grandma's invited to the party and no one wants to think about Grandma and that other thing at the same time.

The Sex/Gender Distinction

This contrast between the social and the biological is referred to as *the sex/gender distinction*. Sex has to do with your reproductive organs; it's what we as a species share in common with all other animals that come in a male and female variety. (Most obviously: penises and vaginas.) Gender has to do with how we socially complex humans respond to these biological realities. This is sometimes captured in the slogan "Gender Is the Social Interpretation of Sex." And our culture has some very definite ideas about what this social interpretation is supposed to consist of—what people are supposed to look like, what we're supposed to want, and how we're supposed to act is decided by what our genitals are presumed to look like.

The quickest way to learn what these very definite ideas are is to look at gender stereotypes. The feminist point here isn't that there aren't any exceptions to gender rules; it's to get straight on what the rules are, so that we can start breaking them with impunity. As we all know, there are exactly two options here: masculinity and femininity.

The battle of the sexes can heat up pretty quickly when you start laying the stereotypes out. Men are supposed to be logical and level-headed but emotionally stunted, while women are supposed to be intuitive and emotionally savvy but also veer toward irrationality and being kind of crazy. Men are supposed to be strong, independent, and practical, while women are supposed to be weak, needy, and frivolous. Men never ask for directions, and women can't drive. Men don't listen, and women never stop talking. Men can't remember to put the toilet seat down if their life depended on it. Women will remember that time you forgot their birthday back in the first Bush administration. Women want flowers and chocolate and romance; men's version of Valentine's Day is steak and a blowjob.

When we don't pay attention to the sex/gender distinction, we imply that whether you have a penis or a vagina will *necessarily* determine what kind of person you are. Of course, real people are much more complex and varied. But femininity and masculinity are the only two gender options available to people in most cultures, and their parameters are clearly defined. These two genders are usually thought to map directly onto sex: biological males are expected to have masculine characteristics and biological females feminine ones. The technical term for the view that men and women have distinct and different qualities or essences that derive directly and naturally from their different biological makeups is *gender essentialism*. In this view, gender differences are viewed as universal, innate, and unchanging.

For a very long time we've pretended that this is just the way things are, that men are indeed from Mars and women from Venus. Gender essentialism is as old as Western culture itself— we see it in writings dating even further back than ancient Greece. The Christian tradition then picked the choicest misogynist elements of the classical Greek and Jewish traditions and expressed them in the story of Adam and Eve. The theological doctrine that God created two sexes with immutably distinct natures remained the dominant view until Darwin published his work on evolution in the mid-nineteenth century. And even this new scientific doctrine left the underlying belief that men and women are fundamentally different untouched, merely telling a different story about how these essential differences developed. These interrelated orthodoxies continue to influence how we think about sex and gender to this day.

The Historical Roots of Sex and Gender

The ancient Greeks had some seriously wacky beliefs about the birds and the bees. Lacking the scientific knowledge we take for granted today, they didn't split the sexes up the way we do. Instead, their understanding of human nature depicted men as true human beings and women as deformed or mutilated versions of the real thing. Women are defective and inferior by nature, Aristotle claimed. He thought women had the same genitalia as men, but their ovaries were deformed testes that had found their way inside their bodies. (We also had fewer teeth, apparently.) Because they were deficient in the "vital heat" necessary to produce semen, he believed women were able to serve only as vessels for growing the offspring that propagated from men's seed; women provided the "matter" for reproduction, while men provided the "form." Women's lack of vital heat also had implications for their characters, Aristotle thought, making them naturally less intelligent than men, more passive,

> more mischievous, less simple, more impulsive ... more compassionate ... more easily moved to tears ... more jealous, more querulous, more apt to scold and to strike ... more prone to despondency and less hopeful ... more void of shame or self-respect, more false of speech, more deceptive, of more retentive memory [and] ... also more wakeful; more shrinking [and] more difficult to rouse to action.[1]

These views about what women are like are literally thousands of years old, and yet they sound like something you could read today, and not just on an incel subreddit.

We might've wised up in our understanding of biology since the days of the ancient Greeks, but the essentialist belief that women's biology makes them naturally inferior to men has stuck around. We still tend to think of women as beholden to biological forces in ways that men are not, held hostage to our hormones, powerless in the face of the irrational whims of PMS. More than a few voters admitted to refusing to vote for Hillary Clinton because they were worried she'd start WWIII when she had her period. (This is especially rich given that her own husband's failure to keep his hormonal urges in check almost took down his presidency, but no one seems to think men's inability to keep it in their pants should disqualify them from elected office.) Simone de Beauvoir criticized this tendency to paint women alone as "think[ing] with [their] glands": "Man superbly ignores the fact that his anatomy also includes glands, such as the testicles, and that they secrete hormones. He thinks of his body as a direct and normal connection with the world, which he believes he apprehends objectively, whereas he regards the body of woman as a hindrance, a prison, weighed down by everything particular to it."[2] The perniciousness of gender essentialism, then, isn't just that it portrays the two sexes as inherently different. It's also that, *from the very beginning*, it has depicted the female sex as inferior.

Religious Orthodoxy

The Judeo-Christian religious tradition picked up and ran with these ancient ideas about what men and women are like. Along the way, even nastier ideas were thrown into the mix, particularly that of women as sexual temptresses responsible for the downfall of humanity. By the time these theologians had finished working their magic, women's inferior social status would no longer be seen merely as a biological inevitability, but as a state of affairs that had been divinely ordained.

According to the creation story found in Genesis, God created Adam to have dominion over all of nature, and created Eve to serve as a helper for him. There's a clear hierarchy here, with God as head honcho, Adam as steward, Eve as the steward's assistant, and then all the other creatures that apparently need to be taken care of.* Being created out of Adam's rib, instead of directly from the breath of God, symbolizes woman's inferiority to man—Eve is a less perfect approximation of God than Adam, being, as she is, one step removed. The belief that women are imperfect humans is built right into this creation story: men are created in God's image, while women are cheap knockoffs.

Also worth pointing out is that Adam and Eve are unashamed of their nakedness while they're in the Garden of Eden. This state of undress symbolizes their innocence: like children, they don't yet know about sex, or, for that matter, about the difference between good and evil. Everything changes, of course, when Eve strikes up a conversation with a snake, who convinces her to eat fruit from the forbidden Tree of the Knowledge of Good and Evil. She convinces Adam to eat it too, and after one bite of the fateful fruit, the jig is up.

We see in the story of the Fall a picture of women as gullible and manipulable, but also as dangerous and manipulative. The serpent picks Eve as his mark because he knows Adam is too smart to fall for his tricks. But while he might be able to see through the

---

* All the climate change and environmental degradation and mass extinctions and whatnot suggest we stewards are doing a *very bad job*. But I digress.

serpent's cunning, Adam can't withstand his wife's wiles. Here we see the archetype of women as temptresses whose unbridled sexuality threatens to be responsible for men's downfall. And we see the idea that women's sexuality is dangerously tempting to men and in need of male control. These ideas are behind the various religious practices that valorize feminine modesty and make women answerable for men's lust, those that hold women responsible for averting men's gaze by covering their hair with veils or wigs and their bodies with modest clothing.

Eve was guilty of vanity in thinking that she could be like God, and of being insufficiently obedient to God and to her husband. Like all women after her, she is uppity and in need of discipline from her betters. Because she doesn't know her place, God concocts a set of punishments designed to ensure that she'll never forget it. Because Eve was created to be Adam's helper, her punishment is to be even more subordinated than she already was, and to be defined primarily in terms of her capacity to bear children for him. (Anyone who has experienced the excruciating pain of childbirth can attest that being told that it's a punishment from God for the insubordination of your arrogant forebears is unquestionably the single worst bit of religious dogma ever concocted. Seriously, this is how you make sense of this phenomenon? You tell women that it's their fault for being descended from a disobedient brat who didn't know her place? And then you compound the insult by insisting that it's also been divinely ordained that they be ruled over by their husbands?)

Adam, comparatively speaking, gets off easy. Losing your immortality and being sentenced to a hardscrabble life of suffering isn't exactly awesome, either, but remember that women are condemned to all this as well, plus more. Basically, Adam gets kicked out of his parents' basement and told he has to grow up and get a job, while Eve has to submit to this loser plus endure the added indignity of brain-melting pain while she's having his kids.

The story ends with the couple being expelled from the Garden of Eden. Adam takes up the mantle of leadership and steps up and accepts responsibility for ruling over all of God's creation—including his wife. Eve's job is to shut up and submit, and to pump out babies. These roles are reflected in the patriarchal family, where a man is head of his household with the authority and responsibility to lead his wife and his children. The inequality of these gender roles is justified by an essentialist worldview that portrays men as naturally fit to lead and women as naturally fit to follow. Just as Eve couldn't be trusted to keep her hands off the one thing God said she couldn't have, wives can't be trusted to take care of themselves or their children without active leadership from their husbands.*

Interestingly, the other Abrahamic religion, Islam, has an interpretation of this story that is considerably friendlier toward women than the takes traditionally offered up by Judaism and Christianity. Instead of foisting all the blame for the Fall of humanity onto Eve, Muslims believe that Adam and Eve were *equally* responsible for the sin of hubris. This, obviously, is a serious improvement over Judaism's and Christianity's willingness to throw Eve (and all women after her) under the bus. But despite being comparatively cool in at least this regard, Islam still shares the theological doctrine that God created two sexes with immutably distinct natures, revering Adam and Eve as the "father" and "mother" of humanity.

The biblical creation story is responsible for entrenching essentialist understandings of what human beings are like as

---

* In case there's any doubt about this, Paul lays it down in his letter to Timothy: "Let the woman learn in silence with all subjection. But I suffer not a woman to teach, nor to usurp authority over the man, but to be in silence. For Adam was first formed, then Eve. And Adam was not deceived, but the woman being deceived was in the transgression." (Timothy 2:11–14)

men and women respectively. There are, of course, much less retrograde interpretations of this story out there than the fairly standard one I've just given you. A variety of progressive theologians have valiantly tried to show how these religious texts can be used to support the equality of the sexes. Whether or not these newer accounts are ultimately successful, the historical influence of this religious tradition remains fairly grim by feminist lights. And even the most radical of theologians would be hardpressed to offer up an interpretation of these texts that doesn't, explicitly or implicitly, establish an equivalence between sex and gender. Sex difference isn't accidental to the creation story. God intentionally made human beings in male and female forms so they could populate the Earth. Traditional understandings of sex and gender are thus fundamental to this story about what it means to be human.

We're still feeling the effects of this story, not least because this religious picture of humanity consisting of two dichotomous sexes would be picked up and ensconced by modern science.

Scientific Orthodoxy

Charles Darwin's nineteenth-century theory of evolution successfully overturned centuries of religious dogma. His theory's two central theoretical breakthroughs were the processes of natural and of sexual selection. Natural selection explains how successful species adapt to their environments, the thought being that "survival of the fittest" means the individuals best suited to their environment will be likelier to survive and pass their traits on to their offspring. Sexual selection, by contrast, focuses on the particular adaptations that result from successful mating strategies, the thought being that individuals with traits that attract the most mates will be likelier to produce more offspring, and so the traits that aid in reproductive success will be inherited across generations. We are the way we are, in this picture, because our hominid ancestors spent millennia working out the kinks for us. (Thanks, *Homo erectus*. Walking upright is awesome.)

Notice that this Darwinian picture also, in its own way, makes sexual difference fundamental to our understanding of what we are as a species. Males and females are inherently different because of our different reproductive roles. Darwinian evolution was first controversial in part because it upset the idea that the human form is necessary and divinely ordained—instead of being made in God's image, it turns out we're just as much the result of random chance as is every other creature, and all of us could have been otherwise. But even though the theory of evolution introduced a novel degree of contingency into our sense of who we are, some things seem a lot more contingent than others. It's easier for us to imagine that humans might have evolved in divergent ways when it comes to characteristics like walking upright or having ten fingers and toes than it is to imagine that we might have evolved into a species that doesn't reproduce sexually.

We can head back even further than your high school bio classes, to those super-awkward talks about the birds and the bees your parents subjected you to when you were a kid. Again, sex differences probably featured pretty heavily. The picture was relatively simple at first. Boys have penises and get to pee standing up, girls have vaginas and have to sit down. As you grew older, more details were added. Adult male bodies have penises, testicles, big beefy muscles, low voices, body hair. Adult female bodies have vaginas, breasts, baby-making equipment like uteruses and ovaries, less muscle mass and more body fat, higher voices, and less body hair. These sex differences are genetic (males have XY chromosomes, females have XX chromosomes) and they're hormonal (males have more testosterone, females have more estrogen and progesterone). And, again, we are this way because for millions of years all the hominids who came before us figured out that this is the only way to make more hominids.

If we weren't psychologically complex social hominids, this would be the whole story. Gender wouldn't exist. Humans would just exist in two sexes (what you call "dimorphic") running around trying to pass on their genes by having as much sex as possible with members of the opposite sex, like most of the other beasts in the jungle. For the longest time, scientists didn't bother to separate sex and gender because everyone thought they amounted to the same thing. Then, in the 1960s, psychologists studying trans people fastened on the term "gender" (heretofore used only to refer to masculine and feminine words like the Italian *lui* and *lei*)[3] as a conceptual tool for explaining why trans people so often described feeling like they were "trapped in the wrong bodies:" their gender didn't match up with their sex.[4] It's now commonplace for scientists to admit that the cultural can be analyzed separately from the biological. Still, even though sex and gender are now regarded as conceptually distinct, scientific orthodoxy generally continues to map them onto each other in a one-to-one correlation. Scientific theories about how this works fall into two camps: determinism and interactionism.

According to determinism, sex *directly causes* gender: biological differences associated with our differential reproductive capacities (i.e., sex differences) generate psychological and social differences in how we behave and interact (i.e., gender differences). So biological males will necessarily display masculine character traits, and biological females will necessarily display feminine character traits. While determinism was long the received view, almost no scientist buys it anymore, in large part because it takes exactly one disconfirming instance—one masculine female or one feminine male—to refute it.

Interactionism is now the much more commonly held scientific view, according to which biology and culture *interact* to govern human behavior. Determinism holds that the direction of explanation generally goes one way only: biological sex differences give rise to gender differences. Interactionism, on the other hand, says the direction of explanation can go both ways and is thus far more amenable to feminist concerns about gender essentialism. Feminist interactionist neuroscientists such as Lise Eliot caution against too quickly assuming that sex differences arise solely from biology. "Who's to say," Eliot asks, "that such differences are caused by nature and not by learning— by the thirty or so years of living as a male or female that any research subject invariably carries into the MRI scanner?"[5] Feminist interactionist psychologists such as Cordelia Fine further debunk the idea that there are hardwired differences between male and female brains, drawing on what science has discovered about the plasticity of our brains in responding to our environments to demonstrate the absurd oversimplification involved in pretending that little Johnny is biologically destined to play with trucks and little Suzie with dolls.[6]

With the rise of interactionism, many scientists are finally coming around to a realization that feminists have been trumpeting for decades. "Socialization molds our bodies," wrote Marilyn Frye in 1983, "enculturation forms our skeletons, our musculature, our central nervous system. By the time we are gendered adults, masculinity and femininity *are* 'biological.' They are structural and material features of how our bodies are."[7] The relationship between sex and gender is far more complicated than we used to think it was. But not everyone's gotten the memo, unfortunately. Scientists frequently still espouse laughably simplistic versions of gender essentialism. Far too many evolutionary psychologists, for example, tend to cling to a just-so story that insists that men want as much no-strings-attached sex with as many different attractive ladies as possible while women yearn for commitment from a single dude with as much status (read: money) as possible. Insisting that they're merely describing the soundest evolutionary strategies for beings who play different biological roles in reproduction, they too often cherry-pick data that just happens to fall in line with and justify the patriarchal status quo.[8]

Even though we're making progress, people's "common sense" still stubbornly insists that there are far more fundamental, unchangeable differences between men and women than is actually the case. An idea that's this deep-rooted will survive in the face of an awful lot of evidence to the contrary. We've just taken a glimpse at the long and illustrious history of this ill-gotten belief. Gender essentialism has been so taken for granted in Western culture that it wasn't until the middle of the twentieth century, when de Beauvoir wrote that "one is not born, but rather *becomes* a woman," and that "social discrimination produces in women moral and intellectual effects so profound that they appear to be caused by nature,"[9] that it started to dawn on us that there might be other explanations for why men and women seem to be so different.

Feminism and the Social Construction of Gender

Following in de Beauvoir's footsteps, many feminists have been extraordinarily critical of gender essentialism. They argue that differences between how men and women act can be explained by differences in how we are socialized. Many have been willing to admit that there are some biological differences between men and women—most men have penises, most women have vaginas, for example—but argue that any behavioral differences we see are because of the gendered social roles we have little choice but to take on.

Although de Beauvoir's 1949 *The Second Sex* was the first feminist tract to discuss the social construction of masculinity and femininity at length, she didn't actually use the term "gender" in her analysis. It was the feminist scholar Gayle Rubin who coined the phrase "the sex/gender system" in 1975, defining it as "the set of arrangements upon which a society transforms biological sexuality into products of human activity, and in which these transformed sexual needs are satisfied."[10] Drawing on the work of others who were also writing at the time, Rubin formalized a picture—one that rejects the idea that our character is biologically determined but sees bodies themselves as biologically given—that would hold sway among feminists and other gender theorists for decades to come.

The feminist theorist Linda Nicholson describes the basic picture here as a "'coatrack' view of self-identity," where "the body is viewed as a type of rack upon which differing cultural artifacts, specifically those of personality and behavior, are thrown or superimposed."[11] This picture of the relationship between biology and society explains why biology needn't completely determine what women must be like, even while women experience similar biological demands. The shape of a coatrack will constrain what can be tossed on it—it's not like anything will fit—but it still leaves room for a great deal of variety. Feminists were drawn to the coatrack view because it allowed them to make sense of how the options for acceptable presentations of femininity have been shaped by the sexist norms of patriarchal societies, while leaving open the possibility that if we change these societies for the better this will change women's personalities and behaviors for the better.

So what does this socialization look like? Think about some of the differences between the sexes that are usually chalked up to biology, claims such as that men are naturally physically stronger and more muscular than women, or that women have naturally less body hair than men. Then spend five minutes at a gym or waxing studio and watch the crazy amount of time and money and energy people are willing to put into making their bodies conform to what they're already supposed to look like naturally. Men grunt away in the weight room and try to remember to take an occasional break from the gun show to throw in a leg day once in a while. Women trot on cardio machines like hamster wheels and assiduously avoid lifting anything heavier than eight pounds, lest their arms stray from Michelle Obama's gorgeously toned specimens to the dreaded "bulky." Sometimes I think that if women were really being honest on dating sites or social media, our number-one hobby would be "body hair removal." Guys, I assure you, you have no idea how much time and energy we women pour into maintaining the illusion that we're naturally hairless. Whole technologies, whole industries, exist completely outside your awareness: hard waxing, soft waxing, hot waxing, sugaring, threading, depilating, tweezing, shaving, lasering, bleaching, industrious little fairies who'll harvest your pubes to line their enchanted nests. (OK, I made that last one up.) The point here is that even if there are a few biological differences between men and women, they're dwarfed by the juggernaut of socialization that goes into exaggerating them.

And this socialization begins *early*. The second we find out a baby's sex—either from ultrasounds, prenatal genetic testing, or once the baby is born—what sex we think they are determines how we treat them. If you want to test this out, I highly recommend dressing your infant in green or yellow and letting an acquaintance hold them while you refuse to divulge the baby's sex. I did this a few times when my daughter was small. When asked if she was a boy or a girl, I'd reply, "Yep!" and then sit back with a bag of popcorn and enjoy the befuddled show. Even seasoned baby snugglers would find themselves at a loss. If you don't know whether babies are boys or girls, you don't know whether to bounce and jostle and lower your voice and call the baby "Buddy," or to gently cradle and rock them and raise your voice and coo, "Pretty Girl!" Most of the time we don't realize we're sustaining gendered behavior, of course. It's only when we're not given the appropriate gender cues that we notice how much we were depending on them.

In 1978, sociologist Nancy Chodorow enriched earlier feminist accounts of the social construction of gender by hypothesizing that gender develops as a response to traditional parenting practices.[12] It matters that it's women, and not men, who are almost always the primary caretakers of very small children, Chodorow argued. When infants are born they don't have a conception of themselves as distinct from their caregivers—that sense of individuality doesn't fully come online until closer to age three. Kids are predisposed to identify with their caregivers, and the developmental process of maturation is, in part, a process of coming to understand oneself as a separate individual. But because a mother is herself likelier to identify with her daughters than with her sons, she will unconsciously encourage her sons to psychologically individuate themselves from her, and unconsciously discourage her daughters from doing so. This prompts the development of ego boundaries that are clear and rigid in boys and flexible and blurry in girls. By adulthood, this looks like stereotypically gendered behavior: clingy and needy women whose confused ego boundaries mean they have difficulty differentiating their own interests and well-being from that of their children and partners, and cold and self-reliant men whose well-defined ego boundaries mean they have no trouble prioritizing their own needs and interests over anyone else's. Whether or not we want to buy into the psychoanalytical details of Chodorow's account (there are an awful lot of Freudian ideas underpinning her theory), the thought that people are profoundly affected by the early relationships they have with their caregivers seems plausible.

As kids grow older, the gendered treatment continues. Girls' hair is grown long, adorned with uncomfortable barrettes and braids and bows and requiring extensive daily maintenance that trains girls to accept the sacrifices and discomforts of femininity. In contrast, boys' hair is trimmed short and kept easily manageable. Girls are given baby dolls and princess clothes and toy kitchens while boys are given trucks and dinosaurs and action figures. (They're not dolls! They have guns and kill things!) Girls are dressed in scratchy lace, cumbersome skirts, and flimsy shoes while boys' fashion is comfortable and sensible. Girls are coddled and overprotected while boys are roughed up and informed that they don't cry. Girls are shushed when they're noisy while boys' rambunctiousness is written off as inevitable. ("Boys will be boys," after all.) Girls are scolded for being bossy while boys are praised for their budding leadership skills. And again—it doesn't matter whether you're a woke feminist who's enlightened about these forces of socialization or not. You might avoid some of the more egregious instances of this enculturation, but you still treat kids differently depending on their perceived gender. We can't help ourselves. Hell, I've noticed myself doing it with cats.

Gender is one of the first social categories we give to kids, and they learn to be awfully good at policing it. The developmental story has more room than you might think: kids start to pick up that there are such things as girls and boys around two or three. But it isn't until around age five that they figure out that gender identity (their own and others') is supposedly fixed. So there's this window where they've learned that gender is a really important category—even more important than colors and shapes and farm animals and all the other things we like to drill them on so incessantly. Kids are smart. They've picked up all the social cues and gotten the message that we *really* care about gender, so they don't want to mess this one up. And they think it's something they really could get wrong. They think that being mistaken for the wrong gender will actually change what gender they are. But before five they don't fully understand that if they're a girl they can be a firefighter or a truck driver or the president when they grow up, but they can't be a daddy.

I remember when my little brother was around three he'd get incredibly upset when our otherwise sweet uncle would tease him by calling him a girl. I was a decade older, and remember thinking, "Jeez, what's the big deal? We all know you're not really a girl, little dude. Chill out!" But it actually makes sense that he'd lose his mind about this, because at three you're still firmly in the process of identity formation, still coming to understand yourself as a distinct individual who's separate from your caregivers. And when you're trying to figure out who you are, and how this identity fits in with those around you, of course it's upsetting when someone starts messing with a concept that feels so tenuous to you. Kids in this stage tend to cling to gendered categories as if their little lives depend on it. They like the world around them to be black and white. (Or pink and blue, as it were.) This explains why they can get so obsessed with reveling in gender, why they tend to perform it so hyperbolically. Toy manufacturers have wised up to the market possibilities of this developmental stage where kids feel like they have to prove that they're girls or boys: you can sell twice as much plastic crap if boys and girls refuse to play with each other's toys.[13]

Kids, it turns out, are basically wee Judith Butlers. Gender, Judith Butler argues, is fundamentally a *performance*—one that is perhaps more thoroughgoing but no less artificial than the fabulous hyperbolic parodies served up by drag queens.[14] Our gender isn't a deep-rooted ontological fact about us; it's something we *do,* executed via our mannerisms, our costumes, our comportment. Kids at this developmental stage tend to be little gender police because they get that there's nothing behind the smoke and mirrors, nothing to gender above and beyond what the audience thinks of the show.

An upshot of this realization, Butler thinks, is that we should stop taking gender so seriously, take a lesson from drag queens who take such delight in messing with these categories and their boundaries, and understand that none of the rules of gender are inscribed on a stone tablet somewhere. "Perhaps the main difference between heterosexuals and queers," muses Marilyn Frye in the same vein, "is that when queers go forth in drag, they know they are engaging in theater—they are playing and they know they are playing."[15] Butler asks queer people to revel in their disruption of the heteronormative status quo, to take pride in their ability to expose gender as the performance it is. But although Butler believes that all the world's a stage, she doesn't think the players are necessarily free to choose their parts at will. Gender performances are rooted in a social superstructure, she thinks, one that arises out of zillions of unconscious everyday interactions. We've been playing the gender game so long that it's become our reality; we've repeated the performances so many times that we've forgotten we're acting. Because we no longer see it as a game we think the reason we act as we do must have to do with biology, with a set of incontrovertible facts about our bodies

We treat boys and girls differently from day one, but then turn around and insist that the inevitable differences in their temperaments are simply natural. Girls are just different from boys, we insist. They just *are*. Occasionally I'll have a liberal friend raised on *Free to Be . . . You and Me* confide that they, too, used to be committed to the ideal of gender neutrality, but once they had kids they realized the differences in their dispositions really were ingrained. They bought kitchen toys for their son and he

turned a spatula into a gun! They bought trucks for their daughter and she treated an excavator like a baby doll! They tried
and failed at gender-neutral parenting. Nature is the fallback
explanation—what else could it be?

Like many other feminists, I remain skeptical of this line of
reasoning. I think it's almost impossible to realize just how differently we treat boys and girls. What these well-meaning parents fail to understand is how ubiquitous this socialization is,
and how much of it we participate in unconsciously. We start
gendering our children *in utero*. Parents report gendered hopes
and dreams for their child as soon as they know what the fetus's
genitals are.[16] They use gendered adjectives to describe their
children—boys are labeled as strong, alert, and coordinated
while girls are tiny, soft, and delicate—when infants are twenty-
four hours old.[17] While researchers have found some minor physical differences between girls and boys in infancy—boys tend
to have bigger heads and are a bit fussier—they've also found
that parents frequently see differences that aren't actually there
(falsely predicting the physical precociousness of their sons and
timidity of their daughters, for example).[18]

Something else to remember is that despite our narcissistic
aspirations, we parents are not the only, nor even necessarily
the primary, influences on our kids. Even if they're not getting
gender socialization from us, they're still getting it. Very few
parents spend 24/7 with their offspring these days. Even those
kids whose parents are completely enlightened about gender
are still subject to outside influences from family, friends, and
caregivers who might not share these views. Grandma's not just
spoiling the kids by giving them ice cream for dinner and letting them stay up past their bedtime; she might also be undoing
all the hard work you've put in to protect them from regressive
gender norms. And then there's the media: stereotypical repre-
sentations of gender abound in our cultural narratives. Every

book, every TV show, every iPad app, every movie—almost all of it contains characters following stereotypically gendered scripts. We forget that the world we live in is deeply gendered; we're so far down the rabbit hole that we no longer notice it anymore, much less stop to ask whether we should actually want to be where we are.

An Exception to the Rule

While the overarching trend in feminist scholarship is one that seeks to debunk gender essentialism, there's an exception that bears mentioning. It turns out that not all feminists have been keen to reject traditional understandings of gender. A few, known as *difference feminists*, accept the view that men and women have distinct natures.

Difference feminists shouldn't be confused with conservative or traditionalist adherents of gender essentialism who would have us believe that the character traits of the two genders are complementary and that men and women should occupy traditional patriarchal social roles because society at large and families in particular run more smoothly when everyone stays in their lane and sticks to what they're good at. Instead, difference feminists argue that most of the world's ills have arisen because of the many creative ways we've found to overvalue masculinity and undervalue femininity over the years. Not just sexism, but global poverty, war, and environmental degradation could be solved if we pulled our heads out of our collective rear ends and started properly respecting the things women are naturally good at, they think.

In the 1980s, feminist ethicists such as Carol Gilligan and Nel Noddings constructed a new moral theory known as the ethics of care. According to care ethics, women have a "different moral voice" that prioritizes helping and nurturing the vulnerable, appreciates human interdependence instead of fetishizing independence, and understands the fundamental importance of intimate relationships.[19] Gilligan and Noddings both actually retracted the support for the gender essentialism found in their early work, later admitting that the differences in moral reasoning they found between men and women could just as easily be attributed to differences in their socialization. However, at least some theorists who work in the tradition of care ethics remain committed, either implicitly or explicitly, to some version of gender essentialism. The 1980s also saw eco-feminists such as Susan Griffin, Mary Daly, and Starhawk decry dominations of women and nature that they saw as intercon-nected, pointing out how women are seen as more embodied and irrational and defined in terms of the animal function of their reproduction, and how Mother Nature is seen as some-thing to be subdued and dominated in the name of androcentric civilization.[20] Many care ethicists and ecofeminists continue to employ the strategy of reappropriating feminine ideals and characteristics that have historically been denigrated, affirm-ing the idea that men and women are different not in order to defend a sexist status quo but to get us to pay attention to the wisdom women have always had.

Still, for the most part, feminists have been suspicious of gen-der essentialism, for the very good reason that they understand that just as the bullies on the playground take all the good toys and won't let anyone else play with them, our culture has given all the good stuff—all the social power, all the best ways of being human—to the men.

Gender as Reproductive Sales Pitch

On the interactionist picture that holds sway with most scien-tists, remember, gender is what we smarty-pants humans do with our biological reality, how we pick out certain bodily features to carve up our social world and understand our place in it. Because we're psychologically sophisticated enough to be aware of ourselves as distinct individuals and form a whole bunch of navel-gazing opinions about that, gender identification gives us a way to figure out who we are and where we fit in our communities. We learn as kids that performing gender is the socially acceptable way to announce our genitals to others, and by adulthood the message has been so deeply ingrained that it's long since stopped occurring to us that things could be otherwise.

But why does it matter, really? What's the social purpose of being able to easily sort people on the basis of sex? Why do we care so much? A common scientific answer (coming from the disciplines of evolutionary biology and evolutionary psychology) is that gender categorization facilitates some of our most fundamental biological drives: sexual attraction, pair bonding, and, ultimately, reproduction. Classifying other humans according to gender provides an unambiguous social mechanism for marking out those who might be candidates for getting it on. We perform gender to market ourselves to sexual partners, the argument goes.

But if the purpose of gender is just to socially mark who's a potential reproductive partner, then it's doing a horrible job. The gender system does absolutely nothing to weed out people who aren't reproductively viable—either because they're prepubescent, postmenopausal, infertile, already pregnant, or simply not looking to have a baby right now, thank you very much. Sally Haslanger says that if gender is supposed to track differences in reproductive capacities, then we should ditch our current gender categories and adopt ones that actually track what's relevant—categories like pregnant persons, infertile persons, lactating persons, menstruating persons, perhaps lesbian or gay persons.[21] That this perfectly reasonable suggestion likely strikes you as absurd indicates that something else is probably going on.

Let's be honest: gender matters to us even when it isn't germane to reproduction. We expect people to announce their sex to everyone, even those with whom they have no intention of copulating. Students are expected to announce their sex to teachers, celibate priests are expected to announce their sex to parishioners, parents are expected to announce their sex to children. You don't get a pass from gender if you're monogamously married, or if you're infertile, or if you're celibate. You don't get a pass if you're a child who's too young to be sexually active.

Frye points out how weird it is that we're obsessed with being able to easily categorize people according to sex—note the violence and social ostracism rained down on people who can't or won't announce their sex by playing the gender game—but we cling to draconian social taboos about displaying the parts of our bodies that would actually settle the matter.[22] Other animals make it easy to tell who's game for a little reproductive action. From engorged and colorful genitals to mating calls and dances, most animals aren't subtle about announcing when they're looking to get hot and heavy. But we humans play our cards much closer to our chests. Not only do we not have easily discernible physical markers that display our fertility status, but on top of this we insist on playing coy by wearing clothing that hides our sexual organs. Instead of letting it all hang out, we've adopted a rigorous system of social norms that is supposed to code the state of our fertility but in reality is doing a whole lot more.

Gender as Hierarchical

And so, despite what scientific orthodoxy might have us believe, gender isn't really just a social shorthand for marking who's got the relevant parts you need when you're looking to make babies.

Something else is going on. The problem with gender, most feminists believe, is that it's hierarchical. Forget the whole yin/yang, separate-but-equal, different-but-complementary-natures lines of nonsense. Women, as our culture understands them, are inherently inferior.

It needs stressing yet again that there is nothing at all natural or inevitable about this. Back in 1869, John Stuart Mill realized that "what is now called the nature of woman is an eminently artificial thing—the result of forced repression in some directions, unnatural stimulation in others. It may be asserted without scruple, that no other class of dependents have had their character so entirely distorted from its natural proportions ... for the benefit and pleasure of their masters."[23] Women, Mill thought, are basically overcultivated bonsai plants, with those aspects of our characters that benefit or please men overfertilized and the rest either "left outside in the wintry air, with ice purposely heaped all round, ... [or] burnt off with fire."[24] No wonder we end up such freaks of nature, so maladapted to any environment whose primary purpose isn't to benefit or please men. Like it's just some big coincidence that the two most valorized archetypes of femininity are those of women as unthreateningly charming arm candy and women as compassionate nurturing mothers. Men get someone to flatter their ego, or they get someone to take care of them and their progeny. But either way they get something they want.

The feminist theorist Kate Millet called this shocking imbalance out in her influential 1969 book *Sexual Politics*. "Human personality is formed along stereotyped lines of sex category ('masculine' and 'feminine'), based on the needs and values of the dominant group and dictated by what its members cherish in themselves and find convenient in subordinates: aggression, intelligence, force, and efficacy in the male; passivity, ignorance, docility, 'virtue,' and ineffectuality in the female."[25] The problem isn't just that men and women are socialized into different roles,

Millet argued. It's that the roles women are socialized into are subordinate ones. Women learn to be submissive, ignorant, obedient helpmeets for men. In other words, when women act in the ways we're trained to, we reinforce our own domination.

In fact, what it actually *is* to be a woman in patriarchal societies, Haslanger argues, is to be inferior to a man, to be appropriately subject to male power. A woman is someone who is systematically subordinated along economic, political, legal, and social dimensions, and is "marked" for this oppressive treatment by their real or imagined reproductive features. A man, on the other hand, is someone who is systematically privileged along economic, political, legal, and social dimensions, and is "marked" for this advantageous treatment by their real or imagined reproductive features.[26] The very concepts of masculinity and femininity contain within them the notion that women are lesser beings who deserve particular treatment from men who are their superiors. Some of this gendered treatment is solicitous (as seen in the protections of chivalry), some is degrading (as seen in your garden-variety porn), but none of it is the sort of thing that should be going on between human beings who respect each other as actual equals.

Catharine MacKinnon shares Haslanger's feminist goal of eliminating the gendered categories of masculinity and femininity, but has a slightly different understanding of precisely where these categories come from and what's wrong with them. On MacKinnon's account, gender is rooted in our culture's conception of heterosexual sexuality. And heterosexuality, as we understand it, fundamentally involves gendered relationships of dominance and submission. Masculinity is defined as sexual dominance and femininity as sexual submission. What it *is* to be a man is to be the dominant sexual partner; what it *is* to be a woman is to be the submissive sexual partner. Gender is thus "created through the eroticization of dominance and submission.

The man/woman difference and the dominance/submission dynamic define each other. This is the social meaning of sex."[27]

Men are trained to find women's subordination hot, and women are trained to find this same picture—one where men get off on subordinating women—as also hot. Men's and women's sexualities are both defined from a male point of view, Mac-Kinnon thinks, and this masculine conception of sexuality is imposed on women—by force if necessary. But for both sexes the fundamental incentive to play along with gender is erotic. It's news to no one that sex sells, that we're highly motivated to do what we need to do to get it: even, apparently, acquiesce in our own subordination. So for MacKinnon, the problem with gender isn't merely that it's hierarchical, it's that the particular kind of hierarchy found in traditional constructions of gender is one that is inextricably bound up with sexual violence.*

In case any of this strikes you as hyperbolic, as maybe having been the case thirty, fifty, one hundred, or two thousand years ago but surely no longer applying today, remember that until very recently adult women in the West were considered to be the legal wards of their fathers and then their husbands. This second-class status is symbolized today by the many women who are still given their father's surname at birth and still take their husband's name in marriage. Historically, it meant that women couldn't own property, couldn't vote, and weren't considered to be the heads of their households. We've made some progress, but I doubt you've made it this far into this book with your ability to pretend that all is well and good intact.

Were feminism to achieve its goal of actual gender justice, Haslanger argues, gender itself would be eradicated. Abolishing

---

* If all of this seems a bit hard to grasp at this point, just hold on. We'll return to MacKinnon's influential views on sexual violence in a few chapters.

the sexist social structures that are responsible for sex-marked oppression and privilege would mean that gendered men and women would no longer exist. There'd still be biological males and females (and people in between) in this post-feminist utopia, but these reproductive categories would no longer carry the social importance they do now. They'd end up being closer to how we currently treat matters as trivial as shoe size or blood type—objective facts about a person's body, sure, but not something we generally find all that fascinating or socially important.

Understanding gender as an inherently hierarchical concept means that the world that many feminists hope for will see traditional constructions of gender—that is, masculinity and femininity—eventually disappear entirely. In some ways, we're seeing this start to happen. Traditional gender categories have been loosening their grip, and broadening their scope, for generations now. The increased variety of options for gender expression that are available today is enough to send more than a few conservative tongues a-clucking and heads a-spinning. We have a long way to go, but if feminists like Haslanger and MacKinnon have anything to say about it, this is only the beginning.

CHAPTER 4

THE SOCIAL CONSTRUCTION OF SEX

Feminists have been working tirelessly to discredit our culture's overly reductionist views of human nature since the middle of the last century. And we've made some real progress. There were some glimmers of the conviction that a woman could be destined for more than a second-class life as a baby-making machine before Simone de Beauvoir, but the thought really took off with her insistence that "one is not born, but rather becomes a woman."[1] Feminists in her wake would go on to think through the implications of this claim, replacing a biologically based gender essentialism with the belief that if gendered social roles could be unlearned a more equal world would follow. It became de rigueur to distinguish biological sex from social gender, and the "coatrack view" of the (necessary) body in the grips of (contingent) cultural norms—where the body is a biological given that cultures adorn with different gendered garments (both figuratively and literally)—would hold sway for a solid fifty years.

Feminists embraced the coatrack view because they thought it was the best way to counter biological determinism, the view that biology is destiny. They thought that if we could chalk up the differences between men and women to nurture, not nature, the whole patriarchal house of cards would eventually crumble to the ground. But the coatrack view, it turned out, came with problems of its own.

Feminist Complications of the Nature/Nurture Distinction

Coatrack feminists got a lot of folks on board with their idea that forces of socialization are responsible for the mess we're in, but there remain holdouts who continue to locate men on Mars and women on Venus and refuse to update their address books. Thing is, it'd actually be relatively easy to do the scientific studies that would refute the ideas of these holdouts once and for all. All we'd need to do is raise a bunch of infants from birth in completely controlled environments—like in that old Jim Carrey movie *The Truman Show*. Assign some of the biological males a masculine gender and others a feminine one. Vice versa for the biological females. Get kids from a variety of ethnic backgrounds and raise them in simulations of a variety of cultures, then sit back and record the results.

The problem, of course, is that we'd never get Institutional Review Board approval for this experiment. Ethics boards tend to frown on systematically messing with people without their consent.

"We do not know," reminds Marilyn Frye, "whether human behavior patterns would be dimorphic along lines of chromosomal sex if we were not threatened and bullied; nor do we know, if we assume that they would be dimorphous, *what* they would be, that is, *what* constellations of traits and tendencies would fall out along that genetic line. And these questions are odd anyway, for there is no question of humans growing up *without* culture, so we don't know what other cultural variables we might imagine to be at work in a culture in which the familiar training to masculinity and femininity were not going on."[2]

So what are we supposed to do, given that if we're really being honest with ourselves we should admit that we *know* that we don't know whether it's nature or nurture? I don't know about you, but I'm temperamentally predisposed to catastrophize in situations like this. If you prepare for the worst, everything else is a pleasant surprise, right?*

OK, coatrack feminists asked, so what's the worst thing that could happen if we treat social differences as if they're natural? Well, we risk shoehorning people into boxes they're not happy in by forcing them to live in ways that they'd rather not. We risk channeling people into arbitrary tracks that require them to develop certain talents at the expense of others, regardless

---

* The strategy here is inspired by one suggested by Patrick Grim. Basically, Grim argues that the risks are smaller and the gains greater if we assume that sex differences are social, rather than fundamental, and so insofar as we're ignorant of the actual origins of these differences we should adopt a social explanation for them.

Grim's strategy harks back to Pascal's wager, designed by the seventeenth-century French philosopher and mathematician Blaise Pascal to convince people to believe in God. Pascal's wager isn't, strictly speaking, an argument that proves the existence of God. Instead, it's an argument about what we should believe, given that we simply can't know with certainty whether God exists or not. Pascal argues that if you're a betting man you should try to make yourself believe in God and live accordingly. After all, if your belief in God is mistaken and God doesn't actually exist, everything you stand to miss out on is merely finite (orgies, sleeping in on Sunday mornings, the satisfaction of being right when it no longer matters because you're dead, and so on). But if you're right and God does exist, you score infinite gains (eternity in heaven) and dodge infinite losses (eternity in hell). (Later theologians would question whether an all-knowing God would really be happy to grant eternal salvation to someone who believed for such manifestly selfish reasons, but that's somebody else's can o' worms.)

Patrick Grim, "Sex and Social Roles: How to Deal with the Data," in *'Masculinity,' 'Femininity,' and 'Androgyny': A Modern Philosophical Discussion*, ed. Mary Vetterling-Braggin (New York: Littlefield and Adams, 1982), 128–47.

of what they actually happen to be good at. We risk preventing people from achieving everything they're capable of and from living full, flourishing lives. We risk entrenching unfair hierarchies that systematically advantage certain kinds of people and systematically disadvantage others. In short, we risk missing out on the full potential of our species and harming a lot of individual people along the way.

In other words, we risk doing exactly what we've been doing for centuries.

What's the worst thing that could happen, coatrack feminists asked on the other hand, if we changed tacks and started treating differences as if they're social when they're actually natural? Well, we'd risk wasting time and energy, and distributing social resources in the wrong way, by trying to compensate for inequalities that will be inevitable. But honestly, that's it. If sex differences are unavoidable, we'd be tilting at windmills if we tried to change them, but no actual people would be harmed in the process.

In what I like to read as a truly inspiring display of nineteenth-century snark, John Stuart Mill calls BS on those who clutch their pearls about this.

> One thing we may be certain of—that what is contrary to women's nature to do, they never will be made to do by simply giving their nature free play. The anxiety of mankind to interfere in behalf of nature, for fear lest nature should not succeed in effecting its purpose, is an altogether unnecessary solicitude. What women by nature cannot do, it is quite superfluous to forbid them from doing.[3]

Seriously, though. What, exactly, is the point of forcing people to do things you think they're going to do anyway? What's the point of preventing people from doing things you think they're incapable of? It's almost as if those who are committed to a worldview with traditional gender roles where women exist to be subservient to men don't really believe these things are written into the fabric of the universe but instead know on some level that the only way women are going to put up with it is if they have no other options. Mill's got shade on this too:

> The general opinion of men is supposed to be, that the natural vocation of a woman is that of a wife and mother. I say, is supposed to be, because, judging from acts—from the whole of the present constitution of society—one might infer that their opinion was the direct contrary. They might be supposed to think that the alleged natural vocation of women was of all things the most repugnant to their nature; insomuch that if they are free to do anything else— if any other means of living, or occupation of their time and faculties, is open, which has any chance of appearing desirable to them—there will not be enough of them who will be willing to accept the condition said to be natural to them. If this is the real opinion of men in general, it would be well that it should be spoken out. I should like to hear somebody openly enunciating the doctrine (it is already implied in much that is written on the subject)— "It is necessary to society that women should marry and produce children. They will not do so unless they are compelled. Therefore it is necessary to compel them."[4]

Much has changed in the century and a half since Mill wrote these words. Women unquestionably have more social freedoms than we did in his day. But coatrack feminists insist that we'd be kidding ourselves if we pretended that we don't still spend an awful lot of time and energy policing the social norms that enforce gendered behaviors.

The dangers of getting it wrong about gender essentialism, coatrack feminists demonstrate, fall into two categories: inefficiency and injustice. If we mistakenly assume that gender differences are social when they're actually natural, we create a few inefficiencies. On the other hand, if we mistakenly assume that gender differences are natural when they're actually social, we force people to live miserable lives and unfairly advantage some people at the expense of others, limit the potential of the human species, and create serious injustices. It's important to disambiguate these concerns because what's most efficient might not be what's most just.* Unless we're complete jerks, we should probably agree that justice should generally trump efficiency. So, if push comes to shove, we might want to tolerate some inefficiency in the name of justice. But it doesn't even look like it'll come to that, because there are potential losses of efficiency on both sides, but potential losses of justice only if we treat social differences as if they're natural.

This little exercise in doomsday reasoning suggests that given our state of admitted ignorance it's best to assume that sex differences are the result of nurture, not nature. It bolsters the case of all those coatrack feminists who've jumped on de Beauvoir's anti-essentialist bandwagon over the years. It tears to shreds the idea that women are naturally fit for subjugation. And it vindicates the feminist strategy of fighting sexism by putting the forces of sexist socialization on trial....

Or does it? What if we've been caring about the nature/nurture debate so much because we think it will solve problems it's not actually equipped to settle? This is what the philosopher Louise

---

* Chattel slavery proved to be excellent for the early American economy, after all.

Antony suspects.* She thinks we fixate on the nature/nurture question because we believe its answer will tell us what we should do about sex differences. But the mistake we're making here, she warns, lies in thinking that if gender differences are natural, then they're either good for us or we're stuck with them, and that it's only if these differences are social that they're malleable and up for grabs.[5] "Natural," it turns out, is an awfully slippery word.

"Natural" has multiple meanings. Calling something "natural" can mean it's the way things are without human intervention—like when we try to protect the unspoiled wilderness of the "natural" world from evil developers. Calling something "natural" can mean it's good for us—like when we pay twice as much for products at Whole Foods because their label says they're "natural." Calling something "natural" can mean it's impossible to change—like when we say that it's "natural" for mules to be infertile. Calling something "natural" can mean it's an integral part of a functioning ecosystem—like when we say that tigers have no "natural" enemies. Calling something "natural" can mean it's functioning in a normal, species-typical way—like when we say that it's "natural" for human beings to walk on two legs and to not fly. Calling something "natural" can mean we think it's just the way things should be—like when your drunkle contrasts it with the "unnatural" sex he thinks "the gays" are having.

These different meanings of "natural" are interrelated, and we tend to slip back and forth between them when we use the word, but it's important to remember that they're conceptually distinct. After all, my mediocre vision is natural in at least one sense of the word: it's the way my eyes work without intervention (badly).

---

* Full disclosure: Antony was my dissertation supervisor in grad school, all those years ago. Hi, Louise! ☺

But we wouldn't say that it's good for me to not be able to read traffic signs when I'm driving, so my vision isn't natural in that sense. Also it's relatively easy to fix myopia with a pair of glasses, so my vision isn't natural in the sense of being immutable.

Maybe gender differences are similarly biological in origin, but would be comparatively easy to change with a concerted campaign of socialization. Or, conversely, maybe gender differences are social in origin, but changing the historically entrenched norms and institutions that go into constructing and policing gender is going to end up being way harder than shopping online for a cute new pair of Warby Parkers. Antony's insight suggests that even if we could finally solve this nature/nurture business once and for all, it still won't tell us what we should do about gender. This is because descriptive facts about the way things are, by themselves, can't give normative prescriptions about what we should do. (Philosophers call this the *is/ought distinction*, and we get super grumpy when people mess it up.)

Even if there are naturally occurring behavioral differences between the sexes, that doesn't by itself tell us what we should do about them. Maybe the right thing to do would be to embark on a massive crusade of corrective reeducation to compensate the sexes for their respective inadequacies, with the goal of minimizing sex differences as much as possible. Maybe the right thing to do would be to embrace these differences but try to compensate for thousands of years of systematically overvaluing those character traits considered masculine, like independence and rationality, by swinging the pendulum in the other direction and overvaluing those character traits considered feminine, like interconnectedness and receptivity. Nothing about knowing that gender differences are biological in nature would decide in favor of any of these options.

Similarly, *even if* it turns out that gender differences are social in nature, we'd still have to decide what we want to do about them. Maybe it'll turn out that the conventional gender roles our forebears stumbled upon really are the best way to organize ourselves as a species. Maybe the majority of folks would want to adhere to the gender roles they're most familiar with and we'd risk too much social upheaval if we tried to convince them to change. Or maybe the realization that gender is a social construct would inspire a wholesale rejection of gendered roles and we'd all start living fabulously flamboyant lives of gender fluidity.* The point here is that even if we could solve the nature/nurture dilemma definitively, we won't have actually made any progress on the question of how men and women should behave nor on what to do about the problems of sexism.

If Antony is right, then it doesn't matter if gender differences are social or biological. What matters is if they can and should be changed. The nature/nurture debate ends up being a big old red herring.

Feminist Complications of the Sex/Gender Distinction

Complicating the picture even further, many feminists now believe that it's not only the nature/nurture distinction that turns out to be less helpful than we thought, but the sex/gender distinction as well. Contemporary feminists have moved beyond calling out our mistaken tendency to conflate sex and gender to pointing out that the categories of sex and gender themselves aren't as clear-cut as we like to pretend they are. The old coatrack view of sex and gender has been shown to be problematic in a number of ways. Some feminists now criticize it for falsely assuming that all women experience gender in the same ways.

---

* This is the one I'm cheering for, for the record.

Others accuse it of falsely assuming that sex can unproblematically be understood as a purely biological category without cultural or historical dimensions. Still others claim that it's a mistake to think that distinguishing between sex and gender will be politically useful for feminist purposes.

WHICH WOMEN ARE WE TALKING ABOUT, EXACTLY?

The first problem with the coatrack view of gender is that its proponents failed to take into account the racial, cultural, and socioeconomic differences that exist between women. After all, it's all well and good to say that gender is a cultural construct— to agree with de Beauvoir that one is not born, but becomes a woman—but it's a mistake to then go ahead and pretend that cultures construct gender the same way for all people. Let's just say that the sisterhood hasn't always been great about attending equally to the experiences of *all* sisters. But thanks to the work of intersectionalist feminists, we're finally paying attention to what feminists of color have been saying since at least the days when Sojourner Truth had to ask if she, too, counted as a woman: that what it's like to be a woman varies drastically across social lines of race, class, disability, and so on, and that if we try to pretend otherwise we just end up privileging the experiences of the wealthy, white, straight, able-bodied women over the experiences of all other women.

Betty Friedan is often held up as the poster child of this historically blinkered feminism, accused of exhibiting what Elizabeth Spelman dubbed "white solipsism"[6] for pretending that the "problem that has no name" endured by bored suburban white women was shared by, oh, say, the poor women of color they employed as underpaid domestic help. (Women who are worried about putting food on the table don't tend to have the luxury of wallowing in disaffected ennui.) When white feminists like

Friedan assumed the existence of a "golden nugget of woman-ness" shared by all women independently of race and class, what they were really assuming, claims Spelman, was that "the wom-anness underneath the Black woman's skin is a white woman's, and deep down inside the Latina woman is an Anglo woman waiting to burst through an obscuring cultural shroud."[7]

You might think we just need to get over the thought that there's anything like *the* female experience—some shared set of adventures and exploits that every woman will encounter on her journey from diapers to the grave. The search for a shared female experience is dicey at best, fraught with way too many historical examples of coatrack feminists getting it wrong and making things worse for less privileged women along the way. At the limit, these concerns result in the view that the category of "womanhood" itself is fundamentally confused and thus bet-ter abandoned entirely.

This is the view defended by Judith Butler. She seconds Spel-man's concerns, arguing that in attempting to undermine bio-logically rooted gender essentialism, feminist proponents of the coatrack view failed to take differences among women into account and thus inadvertently created new socially rooted definitions of womanhood that were just as problematic. The solution here, Butler insists, isn't to come up with more inclu-sive accounts of the diverse ways there are to be a woman. The problem won't be fixed by what feminist and anticolonialist philosopher Chandra Mohanty has called the "add and stir" approach, which tries to address coatrack feminism's histori-cal exclusion of many women but still takes the experiences of cis, white, straight, able-bodied, middle-class women as the core that's occasionally spiced up with the experiences of more exotic others.[8]

Butler goes even further. There's a reason that after describing gender as fundamentally a performance she counsels people to revel in messing with its scripts, to treat gender as nothing more than an ironic parody. Gender categories need to be taken down a notch, she thinks, but not only because they harm people in all the ways coatrack feminism spends so much time harping on. Butler charges that in their focus on spelling out the harms of gendered socialization, coatrack feminists unwittingly reified the very things they claimed to be criticizing. By demarcating feminism's subject matter—by articulating a category of harms that deserved feminist attention—coatrack feminists inadvertently defined womanhood in a manner that implies that there are right and wrong ways to be a woman.

"Identity categories," Butler argues, "are never merely descriptive, but always normative, and as such, exclusionary."[9] Any attempt to catalog the commonalities among women, in other words, has the inescapable result that there is some correct way to be gendered a woman. This will inevitably encourage and legitimize certain experiences and performances of gender and discourage and delegitimize others, subtly reinforcing and entrenching precisely some of the forces of socialization of which feminists claim to be critical. And, what's worse, it will inevitably leave some people out. It will mean that there are "real" women whom feminism should be concerned about, and there are imposters who do not qualify for feminist political representation. These imposters will be those who don't do womanhood in the right way, either because their personalities are not appropriately feminine (because they're opinionated, abrasive, or uncaring), because their bodies are not appropriately female (because they're trans, intersex, or fall outside the range of acceptable femininity for any one of a number of other reasons), or because they've somehow managed to escape the all-encompassing forces of sexism and aren't actually oppressed (because they're unicorns).* We don't realistically have to worry all that much about unicorns, but the other two kinds of people clearly deserve feminist protection. The mistake of feminists who defend the coatrack view, Butler insists, wasn't that they came up with the wrong definition of womanhood. It was that they tried to define womanhood in the first place.

This is all well and good, you might say, but if there's no such thing as women, not really, doesn't this threaten to undermine the entire feminist project? Feminism is, after all, a movement whose aim is to end the oppression that women face as a group, and unless we have some way of delimiting who counts as a member of this group, we can't make political demands on its behalf.[10] Furthermore, there's a concern that approaches like Butler's (which in academic jargon fall under the category of poststructuralist feminist theory) end up promoting a kind of ironic quietism that lets us forget that there are actual people in the actual world facing actual injustices. In too many places, Butler and her followers seem to suggest that the best we can hope to do is take the piss out of gender by camping up our performances with a wink and a nudge. But there's not much point in working up the energy necessary for political action if, as philosopher Martha Nussbaum charges of Butler's approach, "we are all, more or less, prisoners of the structures of power that have defined our identity as women; we can never change those

---

* Sally Haslanger freely admits that a few of these unicorns might exist and that they wouldn't count as women according to her hierarchical account of gender. But she's happy to let them slip through the theoretical cracks because they'll be exceedingly rare and, by definition, they're living large and don't need help from feminists anyway. See Haslanger, "(What) Are Race and Gender? (What) Do We Want Them to Be?," in *Resisting Reality: Social Construction and Social Critique* (Oxford: Oxford University Press, 2012), 221–47.

structures in a large-scale way, and we can never escape from them."[11] If the problems with sexism boil down to quibbles over language and culture, then concrete socioeconomic issues like the wage gap, female poverty, and sexual violence threaten to fall off feminists' collective radar.[12]

And so many feminists, motivated by the conviction that the point of feminism is to make the world a better place for real live women, do cling to the thought that there are a few things shared in common by all women, despite the legitimate concerns about our historical exclusions. But articulating precisely what these commonalities are turns out to be surprisingly difficult. It requires, I'm afraid, a bit of a deep dive into the murky waters of the philosophy of language.

For my money, the most promising approaches to defining womanhood treat "woman" as what philosophers call a family resemblance concept. Ludwig Wittgenstein, an Austrian-British philosopher writing in the first half of the twentieth century, was the first to suggest that certain concepts lack a determinacy that's fixed and for which you can specify necessary and sufficient conditions.* Wittgenstein pointed to the concept of "game," suggesting that if you look at everything we count as a game,

> you will not see something that is common to *all*, but similarities, relationships, and a whole series of them at that.... Look for example at board-games, with their multifarious relationships. Now pass to card-games; here

* Necessity and sufficiency are logical terms. Necessary conditions are the features a concept *must* have if it is to count as satisfying a condition. Sufficient conditions are the features such that if a concept has *all* of them together, then it counts as satisfying a condition. If you can specify necessary and sufficient conditions for a concept, then you'll have nailed it down with certainty in logical space.

you find many correspondences with the first group but many common features drop out, and others appear. When we pass next to ball-games, much that is common is retained, but much is lost. . . . And the result of this examination is: we see a complicated network of similarities overlapping and criss-crossing: sometimes overall similarities, sometimes similarities of detail. . . . I can think of no better expression to characterize these similarities than "family resemblances"; for the various resemblances between members of a family: build, features, colour of eyes, gait, temperament, etc. etc. overlap and criss-cross in the same way.[13]

You can't give necessary and sufficient conditions for what counts as a game, but we still tend to know one when we see it, in the same way that even though no one in a nuclear family has features that are exactly identical to those of each of its members we can often still see that they're all related. Thinking about concepts as family resemblances shifts the focus from searching for necessary and sufficient conditions to articulating the cluster of features that are jointly sufficient but not individually necessary to satisfy them.

If "woman" is a family resemblance concept, then it's best understood as a cluster of traits the coatrack view has traditionally filed under both sex and gender.[14] There are certain physical features shared by most women's bodies (sexual and reproductive organs such as breasts, clitorises, vaginas, ovaries, uteruses). There are certain biological processes that take place in most of these bodies (puberty, menstruation, sexual arousal brought about by clitoral stimulation, pregnancy, childbirth, lactation, menopause). And then there are the psychological and social implications associated with most of these bodies (fear of walking alone at night, fear of rape, being dependent on or resenting the protections of chivalry) and their biological processes (rituals and taboos around menstruation, obsessions with virginity, expectations of or taboos around breastfeeding, maternity leave or the lack thereof). There are a whole mess of gender-coded objects (clothing, cosmetics, jewelry, tools ranging from blow dryers to blenders); behaviors (deference, politeness, quietness, emotional expressiveness, inhibited physical comportment); and social practices (pronouns and other gendered bits of language, beauty practices, domestic and care work, chivalry).* And finally there are gender attributions (identifying as a woman, having others identify you as a woman). This cluster of traits isn't static; traits can be added or taken away, or can become more or less significant, over time. But all of them, together, make up what it is to be a woman.

You count as a woman, then, if you sufficiently resemble a paradigm case of womanhood. If you tick off all of these boxes you're definitely a woman; if you tick off none, you're definitely not a woman. If you tick off some but not all then, as we'll see, basic decency demands that we defer to your sincere identification. Thinking about gender in this way makes sense of why trans women are women. It makes sense of why you can reject or experience yourself as chafing against many of the expectations of femininity and count as a woman. It makes sense of why you're still a woman if you've had a hysterectomy or you're infertile or if you choose to not have children. It makes sense of why you're a woman if you're lesbian or bi or queer.

Treating womanhood as a family resemblance concept rescues the coatrack feminist strategy of picking out a group of people who are oppressed in similar, if not identical, ways and

---

* To be clear, I (and most other feminists) think this category is what's doing most of the heavy lifting.

of focusing on how social forces make things worse for people in this group in similar, if not identical, ways.

But coatrack feminism faces other, deeper, feminist challenges.

SEX IS ALSO A SOCIAL CONSTRUCTION

Coatrack feminism spilled a lot of ink emphasizing the fundamental contingency of gender, a lot of time decreeing that gendered social roles could (and should) be otherwise. But it's not just gender that's culturally contingent, Butler and others have argued. Because our physical bodies themselves are always embedded in particular cultural contexts, she points out, they must always be understood as imbued with particular cultural meanings. For Butler, sex isn't a clear-cut biological reality any more than gender is. That we imbue certain physiological features with so much cultural significance mirrors the priorities of our culture. Think about how we typically differentiate males from females. We point to the differences in their sexual organs (penises and testicles versus clitorises and vaginas and ovaries and uteruses). We point to how these organs are used in heterosexual intercourse (penetrating versus being penetrated). We point to the different reproductive roles that result from this intercourse (insemination versus bearing children).

But Butler argues that this way of making sense of our bodies is fundamentally contingent. We could have decided, for example, that what's really most important is whether your pubic hair is curly or straight.[15] There's nothing in nature itself that insists that the fundamental division between people is what role their bodies can play in reproduction. There's nothing in nature that demands that we assign social roles on this basis. Just because it's how we've always done it doesn't mean it couldn't be otherwise. Butler asks us to consider whose interests are served in this categorization. Sex distinctions, as much as gender distinctions, are a reflection of the power structures of those who make them.

Of course, literally every human culture that has ever existed has made some kind of distinction between male and female bodies and has assigned gendered social roles on this basis. You might think we're on to something here. You might reasonably object that the male/female distinction carves nature at its joints, as it were—that it's what philosophers call a "natural kind," an unbiased distinction that simply reflects the structure of the natural world. You might insist that this way of understanding human bodies tracks something fundamental about us, something that exists prior to the forces of socialization.

But we can admit that every culture has made some kind of male/female distinction without pretending that every culture has made the *same* male/female distinction. There are subtle but important differences in how biological sex has been understood around the world.[16] Prior to European colonization, for example, many North American indigenous cultures had a category that was neither male nor female but "two-spirited." Those who identified with this category understood themselves, and were understood by others, as half-male and half-female.[17] In certain parts of pre-colonial Nigeria, some people with female genitals occupied the social role of husband and were thus not women in any conventional sense.[18] In present-day India, *hijras* are a third sex made up of phenotypic males who wear female clothing and undergo a sacrificial removal of their penis and testicles.[19] Sex, it turns out, is no more a cross-cultural constant than gender is.

Further evidence that our conventional understandings of sex don't carve nature at its joints come from science itself. Anne Fausto-Sterling, a professor of biology and gender studies, unpacks the complex ways that biochemistry, neurobiology, and social forces interact to produce what she calls a layered model of sex and gender, where our sex isn't determined by just one thing (like possessing a certain combination of chromosomes) and isn't determined in one instant (like conception).[20] Instead, Fausto-Sterling demonstrates how sex results from layers of developmental processes at the embryological level, and the resulting physical permutations don't fall into the neat boxes we try so desperately to shoehorn people into. Scientific consensus now accepts that biological sex is significantly more nuanced than the familiar binary model would have us believe.[21] The possibilities are stunningly varied. A person's sex chromosomes or sex hormones can say one thing, but if they have certain gene mutations or lack the relevant hormone receptors their plumbing can say something else entirely.* In some cases babies are born with ambiguous genitalia, but in other cases adults learn of their "abnormality" only when they seek treatment for infertility or some unrelated medical condition. We're still learning about the variety of "intersex" conditions that are possible, but all of them upset the longstanding belief that there are only two biological sexes.

The shorthand for making sense of all this is to say that sex is

---

* If humans were sexually dimorphic, all people would fall neatly into either "XX" (female) or "XY" (male) chromosomal configurations. It's true that humans are bimodally distributed around XX and XY configurations, but a number of other possibilities exist, including XXY, XYY, and XO (a null chromosome). The relationship between chromosomes and hormones is likewise not as straightforward as many like to think. Some XX people have congenital adrenal hyperplasia, for example, which causes higher production of testosterone that typically leads the person to develop as phenotypically male. Some XY people have complete androgen insensitivity syndrome, where their body produces "typical" male levels of testosterone but their testosterone receptors are insensitive to the hormone, which usually leads the person to develop as phenotypically female.

not binary. Just as gender exists on a spectrum, with pure femininity on one side and pure masculinity on the other and all of
us actual human beings living our lives in different places in the
middle, sex, too, is nonbinary. Pretending that there are only two
options—male or female—is an oversimplification of a biological
reality that is vastly more complex.

As we become more aware of the oppressions experienced by
nonbinary, trans, and intersex people, we can see how assigning
a person's body a particular sex can be just as oppressive and
reductionist as assigning them a gender. By Fausto-Sterling's
estimate, people born with intersex conditions make up around
1.7 percent of the human population, which, philosopher Lori
Watson points out, is roughly equivalent to the percentage of
the US population who use a wheelchair.[22] Even though there's
certainly more we should be doing, we do make a whole host of
accommodations to our social world for people in wheelchairs—
curb cuts, ramps, elevators, and so on. But until recently, most
of us have had a hard time even admitting that people who fall
outside the male/female binary actually exist, and this social
erasure has concrete effects on their well-being.[23]

Feminist Discussions of Trans Experiences

As our understanding of the complexities of human sexuality
improves, the terminology used to map this terrain continues to
develop. It's probably worth laying this out explicitly. Here are
some of the central terms that are currently used to organize
sexuality:

If you're *cisgender*—"cis" for short—the gender with which
you identify matches up with the sex assigned to you at birth.
If you're cis, it very likely hasn't occurred to you that things
could've been otherwise. If you're cis, the social world is set up
to make you feel normal and accepted and comfortable in your

own skin. If you're not cis, on the other hand, you're *gender non-conforming*, and your life hasn't likely been such smooth sailing. You might be *trans*, and identify with the opposite gender from your sex assigned at birth.* Or you might be *nonbinary*: you might be *androgynous* and identify with aspects of both masculinity and femininity, or *gender fluid* and have a gender expression that changes day to day or year to year, or *genderqueer* or *gender nonconforming* and feel most comfortable opting out of any rigid gender identification whatsoever. In any case, there's hell to pay when you're not cis. If you're lucky, all you'll face is a lifetime of side-eye when using public bathrooms.

But chances aren't great that you'll escape so unscathed. Somewhere between 1 in 4[24] and 2 in 5[25] trans people are assaulted each year solely because they are trans. Rates of fatal violence against trans people, particularly trans people of color, continue to rise.[26] (Trans activists use the term "transmisogynoir" to emphasize that the highest rate of violence in the LGBTQ community is faced by black trans women.) People who are gender nonconforming are routinely denied employment, health care, and access to housing and places of worship.[27] Some 49 to 62 percent of gender nonconforming youth are clinically depressed.[28] Trans people denied access to hormone therapy are nearly four times as likely to be depressed as those who do have access.[29] The rates of suicide or attempted suicide approach 50 percent among gender nonconforming people who are younger, homeless, or unemployed.[30] Our culture doesn't like it when people don't play the gender game the way they're supposed to, and folks who can't or won't play the game pay the price.

---

* For precisely the sorts of reasons that problematize the sex/gender distinction that we've just seen, trans activists are moving away from both the older term "transsexual" and the newer term "transgender" in favor of the broader term "trans."

Although we've got a long way to go, there's light on the horizon. More and more protections for trans and nonbinary people are being enshrined into law. Rigorous scientific studies are starting to show what trans folks have known all along, that gender-affirming medical care considerably improves mental health for trans people.[31] The quality and variety of this care are themselves improving. Trans celebrities like Laverne Cox and Janet Mock are shaping up to be this generation's Ellen DeGeneres and Rosie O'Donnell, whose unthreatening visibility in the 1990s ushered in a new era of mainstream acceptance for many lesbian, gay, and bisexual people.

You might think that a shared suspicion of conventional understandings of sex and gender would make feminists and trans activists natural bedfellows. You'd be wrong.

It all started with Janice Raymond's controversial book, *The Transsexual Empire: The Making of the She-Male*, which was published in 1979.[32] Reissued in 1994, the book continues to inspire "gender-critical" or "trans-exclusionary" radical feminists—TERFs, for short.* Raymond's bugaboo was the "medicalization of gender," which is what she thought trans women were up to in attempting to surgically and hormonally create themselves as women. What trans women were really

---

* There's a huge debate over whether the term "TERF" is a slur. Many feminists who hold that trans women do not deserve feminist protections prefer to call themselves "gender-critical." But Rachel McKinnon argues convincingly that the term is descriptively accurate—that these are, after all, radical feminists who exclude trans people—and, as such, is not a slur. See McKinnon, "The Epistemology of Propaganda," *Philosophy and Phenomenological Research* 96, no. 2 (2018): 483–89.

I submit that if the label is problematic at all, it's because those to whom it applies cannot properly be called *feminists*. You can't be a feminist if you don't care about all women. And trans women are women.

motivated by, she claimed, was the good old-fashioned patriarchal desire to control women, this time by trying to surgically create them. Raymond didn't pay much attention to trans men, bothering only to pigeonhole them as confused and pathetic gender-variant women who could be understood by patriarchal society only if they presented as men, or as unpleasantly aggressive wannabe alpha males. The full brunt of her ire was reserved for trans women. In an early precursor to the recent "bathroom wars," Raymond painted trans women as men who were trying to invade female spaces, trying to "colonize feminist identification, culture, politics and sexuality."[33]

There's a reason many now consider the book to be hate speech. *The Transsexual Empire* was based on Raymond's PhD dissertation, written under the supervision of radical ecofeminist Mary Daly. Daly's bizarre view of trans women was that they are "Frankensteins"—"necrophiliacs"—bent on killing their own life force so they could have sex with it.[34] Raymond was prone to similar hyperbole, claiming, for example, that "all transsexuals rape women's bodies by reducing the real female form to an artifact, appropriating this body for themselves.... Transsexuals merely cut off the most obvious means of invading women, so that they seem non-invasive."[35] You can still find TERF vitriol of this caliber in a lot of spaces online, but in an attempt to present their view as something the respectable public should take seriously, some "gender-critical feminists" have gotten better at toning it down.

Tensions have been broiling ever since, igniting, for example, at the 1991 Michigan Womyn's Music Festival. This lesbian-identified women-only music festival was founded in 1976, moving in 1982 to its permanent 650-acre location in western Michigan. At its peak in the 1990s attendance swelled to more than 10,000 women, who over the course of up to six days each year would listen to music of all kinds, attend intensive workshops, and generally revel in feeling—for many the first time in their lives—completely free from the pressures and dangers of being around men.[36] Friends who attended over the years tell me it was magical. The festival was an event by, and for, women alone. The musicians and attendees were all women, sure. But so was everyone else. Every stage was built and torn down by women; all lighting and sound systems were run by women; every electrician, mechanic, security officer, and doctor was a woman. Women cooked meals for thousands over open fire pits; women provided mental and physical health care, childcare, and ASL translation at every performance. There were sweat lodges, AA meetings, camping resources for disabled women, and a tent exclusively for women of color. Childcare was available for all girls and for boys under the age of five, while older boys were sent to the off-site Brother Sun Boys' Camp.

The controversy erupted when a trans attendee named Nancy Burkholder was asked to leave the festival after several other attendees recognized her as trans and expressed discomfort with her being there.[37] No other trans woman was ever asked to leave the festival, and years later the organizers would publicly apologize to Burkholder. Organizers maintained that while the festival was indeed intended to be a gathering for those "womyn who were born female, raised as girls and who continue to identify as womyn," this ideal was to be understood not as a policy nor a ban on trans women but as "an intention for the spirit of [the] gathering."[38]

There might have been no official policy, but the intention was bad enough. The damage had been done. As public outcry gained steam, a protest camp for trans activists was established outside the festival's gates. Negative coverage of the festival escalated in the progressive LGBTQ media. Some performers lost contracts or were forced to cancel appearances, while others were threatened with physical violence and bomb scares.[39] The Human Rights Campaign and other LGBTQ advocacy groups came out against the festival. Trans women started attending in open defiance of the festival's stated intention. Rather than capitulate to the demands of trans activists, the festival shuttered its doors in the summer of 2015. The Michigan Womyn's Music Festival's fortieth year was its last. Those who wanted a space reserved for "womyn-born-womyn" would have to look elsewhere.

By denying the status of "real women" to trans women, TERFs claim they're just emphasizing the importance of affirming the identity and experiences of those who've spent entire lives in women's shoes.* Even feminist icon Chimamanda Ngozi Adichie has echoed this sentiment, claiming, "It's about the way the world treats us, and I think if you've lived in the world as a man with the privileges that the world accords to men and then sort of change gender, it's difficult for me to accept that then we can equate your experience with the experience of a woman who has lived from the beginning as a woman and who has not been accorded those privileges that men are."[40] Trans women are not women, they're trans women, Adichie insists.†

TERFs sometimes claim that trans women are parodies or frauds, complaining that the performances of femininity enacted by trans women are chiefly retrograde stereotypes, caricatures of a femininity designed primarily for the pleasure of men. When Caitlyn Jenner says that she's always felt like a woman, what she seems to mean by this is that she wants to be an airheaded piece of arm candy all dolled up to delight the male gaze. "The hardest part of being a woman," she's infamously quipped, "is figuring out what to wear."[41] It's nonsense like this that motivated Germaine Greer (a classic 1970s second-wave

---

* This, of course, relies on the false assumption that all trans women have lived in the world unproblematically as men at some point in their lives.

† This, of course, relies on the false assumption that all cis women live in the world in the same way.

feminist) to call *Glamour* magazine "misogynist" for honoring Jenner at their Women of the Year ceremony, claiming that the move was tantamount to affirming that with enough plastic surgery a man can "be a better woman" than someone "who is just born a woman."[42]

TERFs complain that the confidence some trans women seem to have in asserting who they are seems for all the world to be fueled by a lifetime of the buttressing effects of male entitlement, and it's hard not to think this is at least partly true in some cases—particularly when this purported entitlement has been magnified by race and class privilege, as it is with Jenner. But trans women don't hold a monopoly on bad behavior. There are jerks everywhere, and it's unfair to paint every trans woman with the same brush. Just as one of the unacknowledged provisions in the invisible knapsack of racial privilege is white people's ability to behave badly without being seen as an embarrassment to their race, when a cis person messes up they're evaluated as an individual, not as a poster child for an entire class of humanity. Trans people deserve the same rights to imperfection, the same rights to not be taken as representative of their social group, as everyone else.

But it's also no coincidence, TERFs claim, that the trans women who get most of the airtime are those whose performances of gender endorse a regressive, man-pleasing version of womanhood. Feminists who've spent the better part of their lives fighting against a world that uncritically affirms gender stereotypes might be forgiven for getting a little resentful about being told that this is what it's "really like" to be a woman. Of course, it's the media we should properly be blaming for this, not individual trans women. In fact, it's a sign of precisely what TERFs are (or should be) critical of—that our culture has narrow and restrictive and oppressive and objectifying understandings of the limited number of ways to be female—that explains why the media coverage looks the way it does. And the trans community is often just as frustrated as TERFs are at the quality of this media representation. There are many diverse ways to be trans, just as there are many diverse ways to be cis, and many of these forms of gender expression don't just blindly affirm the retrograde stereotypes feminists are worried about. It's just that the trans folks with the more boundary-pushing gender expressions don't tend to be the ones with their own reality TV shows.

Honestly, I think trans women actually have a thing or two to teach us, if only we're willing to actually listen. All the way back in 1974, Andrea Dworkin launched an early salvo in what would eventually become the TERF wars, remarking that, "It is commonly and wrongly said that male transvestites[*] through the use of makeup and costuming caricature the women they would become, but any real knowledge of the romantic ethos makes clear that these men have penetrated to the core experience of being a woman, a romanticized construct."[43] Instead of complaining that trans women are cartoons of reality, Dworkin would have us be honest with ourselves about the absurd amount of time and energy cis women are expected to invest in our performances of femininity. If cis women were honest about our participation in the Panopticon's disciplinary practices, we'd admit that if trans women occasionally camp up their femininity a little more than TERFs might like, they're not doing anything we're not just as guilty of. If we don't like what we see when trans women turn the mirror of femininity toward us, we have only ourselves to blame.

Further driving home the importance of not throwing stones

---

* There are some objections that could be made about Dworkin's terminology here—"transvestite" is no longer the preferred nomenclature, and she doesn't disambiguate between male drag queens and trans women—but it'd be anachronistic to get too fussed about it.

when you live in a glass house, Watson points out that when cis women live as cis, they are, whether they like it or not, affirming a world of binary gender identifications, a world of gender stereotypes, a world with a limited number of acceptable ways to be a woman, just as much as any trans woman does.[44] When I, a cis woman, perform my not terribly original rendition of conventional femininity, I am in part saying that this is what women should be like. "In fashioning myself, I fashion Man," the existentialist Jean-Paul Sartre famously said.[45] I might not always like it, but when I present myself in ways that I know others around me will read as female, I'm not only going along with but actually affirming their conventional beliefs about what women are like. (This, in part, is the power of Butler's advice to mess with our performances of gender: doing so unsettles people's unthinking preconceptions.)

If I'm as guilty of entrenching regressive gender stereotypes as anyone else, why do TERFs think it's trans women who are especially culpable for shoring up gender essentialism? Why aren't they going after cis femmes like me too? We might all agree that the goal is to get to a world free of the shackles of conventional gender ascriptions, but that is not the world we currently live in. "The criticism of trans women as failing to act in ways that are consistent with an ideal of liberation from sex and gender," Watson cracks, "is a little like criticizing any of us for making a decent living under capitalism, or investing our retirement funds in the stock market, if the aim of liberation is the destruction of capitalism as a social, political, and economic system. Even Karl Marx had to eat in the here and now."[46]

Thankfully, TERFs like Greer and Raymond are outliers in contemporary feminism. Even Adichie is no TERF: although she thinks their oppression is not the same as the oppression experienced by women who are assigned female at birth, she recognizes that trans women are undoubtedly oppressed and insists that she believes they deserve to be "part of feminism."[47] Most feminists go even further, however, fully rejecting TERF rhetoric and agreeing that trans women are women, full stop.

Philosopher Talia Mae Bettcher shows how trans people are caught in a double bind.[48] If a trans person successfully passes as cis and is later discovered to be trans, they're seen as an "evil deceiver" who has lied about who they really are. Tragically, this discovery often results in sexual violence against trans women, particularly those who work in the sex trade. And what's worse, this violence is seen by many to be justified because the perpetrator can claim to have been deceived and to have resorted to violence only "out of panic." Trans people who are open about being trans, on the other hand, are seen as "make-believers"—cheap counterfeits, pathetically attempting to be something they couldn't possibly actually be. (Feminist suffragists were written off in similar ways, back in the day, their ideas discredited by depicting these women as mannish and deviant and aspiring to be something they could never be—in that case, men.)[49]

But the problem with this view of trans people as either deceptive or pathetic frauds, Bettcher points out, is that it presupposes that there's a real thing that trans women are failing to be. And this starts to sound an awful lot like the biological essentialism that almost all feminists reject.

The current debates over trans women bring us back to the question of whether there are a set of core experiences that make someone who's been born a woman a "real" woman. Is it menstruation or childbirth? Nope—lots of women don't experience those, either by fate or by choice. What about being subject to sexual violence and harassment? Trans women face as much if not more sexual violence than cis women. And surely we don't want to go back to the days of defining women by their hormones or even their chromosomes—if for no other reason than we'd leave out the estimated 1.7 percent of women who are intersex. When a cis TERF complains that trans women haven't had the same experiences as "real" women-born-women, what she's really saying is "Trans women haven't had the same experiences as *women like me.*" If thirty-plus years of intersectional feminism has taught us *anything*, it's that this is precisely the move that feminists need to stop making.

So much the worse for TERFs, there's coming to be a consensus view among feminists today that holds that what's most important is to let all women decide for themselves if they are, in fact, women. Bettcher affirms the importance of this self-identification, reframing the debate over trans identities from a focus on metaphysical questions about what people "really" are to a focus on ethical and political questions about how people deserve to be treated.[50] She offers an illuminating analogy: when someone says, "I want to go home," it's beside the point to ask whether this utterance is true or false. The point is that they want to go home, and belaboring the question of whether they might be mistaken about this belief of theirs is a dick move that's disrespectful to the point of failing to treat them like autonomous agents. Bettcher claims that there's a kind of "existential identity" over which we have similar authority. This identity is determined not by the kind of empirical facts that could be found on your driver's license but by your answers to existential questions that no one else can decide for you, such as, "What am I about? What moves me? What do I stand for? What do I care about the most?"[51] This existential identity is what trans people are affirming in their gender identification, and questioning their authority to do so by trying to ferret out whether what's in their pants matches their gender identification is morally wrong in the same way it'd be wrong to force someone to convert to a new religion or political party. Feminists have long been pointing out that gender is not simply an imposed social class, it's a lived social identity; it's not just something that is done to us, it's something we do.[52] This has important ramifications for the question of whether it's possible for trans people to get their gender wrong.

The future of the feminist movement is one that includes trans women. TERFs are on the losing side of history on this one. We should do our best to not let this debate devolve into the usual cannibalistic progressive infighting, but it's important for trans-inclusive feminists to stand their ground against TERF discrimination. Properly understanding the history of ideas of how feminists and other gender theorists have progressed in their thinking about sex, gender, and the relationship between them makes clear that the rift that has opened up between TERFS and trans activists is fundamentally misguided, and it's not the trans activists who are in the wrong here. The very same forces that harm women are the ones that harm trans people. This is confirmed by the feminist trans activist Julia Serano, who argues that much of the discrimination faced by trans women has less to do with the fact that they're trans and more to do with the fact that they're willing to unabashedly perform femininity. The problem is less about trans women transgressing conventional gender norms than it's that trans women have picked the losing team: "The fact that we identify and live as women, despite being born male and having inherited male privilege, challenges those in our society who wish to glorify maleness and masculinity."[53]

Feminists and trans activists can't afford to fight amongst themselves. There's a common enemy that we need to unite against.

CHAPTER 5

SEXUAL VIOLENCE

The MeToo movement didn't come out of nowhere. To paraphrase Margaret Atwood, who put it best: Men are afraid that women will laugh at them. Women are afraid that men will kill them. There's a reason one of the central concerns of many feminist theorists and activists is the fact that we live in a culture of sexual violence against women. Feminists refer to this as *rape culture*, a social world in which rape is pervasive and considered to be both normal and inevitable.

This might at first sound extreme. But ask yourself: what are the things I do every day to avoid being raped? Take your time. List them all.

If you're a woman, you probably went on at length: *Don't walk alone at night if you can help it. Be aware of your surroundings. Have a friend watch your drink when you're at a bar so no one slips you a roofie. Go to the bathroom in packs. Have someone you trust walk you to your car at night. Hold your keys between your knuckles so you can use them to punch an assailant if need be. Don't indulge your fantasies of being tied up, because you're not completely convinced you can trust your partner when you're that vulnerable. Always look into your car before getting in, in case someone is hiding in the backseat. Avoid being left alone with that creepy uncle. If you drink in public, make sure at least one of your friends knows to stay with you and take you home if you seem particularly wasted. Acquiesce to your partner's sexual demands when he's had too much to drink or is in one of his moods because you're not certain he won't just do it anyway if you say no. Plan your outfit so that you don't attract the wrong kind of attention and that you're wearing shoes you can run in if necessary. Meet up with your Tinder dates in public spaces. Don't be the only girl out drinking with your group of guy friends, just in case they have too much and get carried away. Carry your phone in your hand when you're walking at night so you can call 911 if you have to. And so on. And so on. Ad nauseam.*

If you're a man, you probably scratched your head for a few seconds and then joked to yourself, "What do I do to avoid getting raped? Huh. Avoid going to prison, I guess."*

Wrap your head around this: the number-one fear that men most have about going to prison is something that women live with every day of their lives.

How many times have you heard someone respond to statistics about women's abuse, rape, harassment, and battery with the insistence that men undergo these harms as well? As if this is some kind of localized skirmish in the war of the sexes, and we're not going to let women win even one single battle? The explanation for this bizarre response, Catharine MacKinnon suggests, is that we don't want to believe the empirical facts about what it's like to be a woman, despite the clear statistical evidence, because we're clinging to the collective belief that men and women really are equal. "This," she says, "is equality for us": a world in which 1 in 6 women will experience rape or

---

* I know this because *every single semester* I pose this question to my students and at least one guy cracks that joke. Don't get me wrong. It's kinda funny. But it's also kind of horrifying.

attempted rape in their lifetime.[1] The statistics for men are strikingly different: 1 in 33 men will experience rape or attempted rape in their lifetime.[2] Hardly equality. Rape is no less tragic for male victims than it is for female victims, obviously, but we shouldn't pretend that the risks are the same for both sexes. They're not.

Rape as Power

In the mid-to-late 1970s the second-wave feminist slogan that "Rape Is About Power, Not Sex" started trickling out into the mainstream, too often accompanied by more than a little willful misinterpretation—the old canard that what feminists really need is to get laid took on the new spin of insinuating that what they needed was a lesson in high school biology. But by insisting that society look beyond the mere biological mechanics of rape, what many feminists at the time were suggesting is that gendered sexual violence is part of a larger cultural picture. Rather than casting it as just an unwelcome penis intruding on an unwilling vagina, these feminists described rape variously as "the perfected act of male sexuality in a patriarchal culture ... [and] the ultimate metaphor for domination, violence, subjugation, and possession," "the paradigmatic articulation of male sexual power as a cultural absolute," and "the symbolic expression of the white male hierarchy ... [and] the quintessential act of our civilization, one which ... is in danger of 'humping itself to death.'"[3] Each of these descriptions urged us to understand the phenomenon of rape not merely as a collection of isolated and unrelated acts of sexual aggression but as interrelated incidents that occur in a broader social and political context—as bars in a birdcage.

The claim that rape is about power instead of sex was articulated most influentially by Susan Brownmiller, whose 1975 book

Against Our Will: Men, Women, and Rape came to be seen by many as *the* feminist take on the subject. Brownmiller's aim was to counter the persistent myths surrounding sexual violence, thus unveiling what she saw as rape's fundamentally political purpose. Rape, she memorably claimed, is "nothing more or less than a conscious process of intimidation by which all men keep all women in a state of fear."[4] Brownmiller insisted that rape's primary function is political, not sexual. Instead of being a natural response to sexual stimuli, she said, rape is provoked by the political motivation to dominate and degrade others. Philosopher Ann Cahill extracts from Brownmiller's work two distinct political functions of rape.[5] First, it can serve as a protection racket. Second, rape can be a way of using women as political pawns.

Understanding rape as a protection racket involves seeing how the omnipresent danger of sexual violence ensures that women need men to protect them from other men. The classic case of a protection racket involves a crime boss who demands payment to "protect" you from the violence he himself intends to visit upon you if you don't pay up. A more common version you might have encountered on vacation is the tourist experience of having kids demand money to "watch your car for you" (from themselves!). What's distinctive about protection rackets is that the threat of violence you're being safeguarded from stems from the very same group of people who are supposed to be doing the protecting. Brownmiller claimed that women's fear of being raped by men—a legitimate fear grounded in statistical empirical reality, not overblown paranoia—makes it difficult or impossible for women to exist in the social world without male protection.

According to Brownmiller, this gendered vulnerability is responsible for, among other things, the institution of marriage. If this allegation strikes you as unromantic or hyperbolic, remember that in most cultures, historically, marriage required a complete abdication of a woman's independence. According to the English legal doctrine of coverture, for example, a woman's legal rights and obligations were subsumed under her husband's. In the words of the eighteenth-century English politician and legal scholar William Blackstone:

> By marriage, the husband and wife are one person in law: that is, the very being or legal existence of the woman is suspended during the marriage, or at least is incorporated and consolidated into that of the husband: under whose wing, protection, and cover, she performs every thing.[6]

Once married, a woman could no longer own property nor make contracts in her own name. Analogous laws existed outside the English common law system: the Roman-Dutch "marital power" doctrine treated women as minors under the guardianship of their husbands; the Napoleonic code subordinated married women and children to their husbands' or fathers' authority; and the American "head and master" laws gave husbands final say over all household decisions and jointly owned property without needing their wives' knowledge or consent. Many of these laws remained on the books well into the twentieth century. Under these various laws women literally *ceased to exist* as independent beings once they were married. This civic erasure was symbolized, in part, by a woman taking her husband's surname.

Why on earth would anyone in their right mind assent to such terms? Ignoring (or minimizing) the many other forms of social ostracism and exclusion unmarried women would have been subject to, Brownmiller believed that the only reason a woman could have to accept such a contract, one that required her to disappear from public existence and rendered her completely dependent upon the vagaries of her husband's goodwill, was her need for protection against rape.

The second way rape functions politically, according to Brownmiller, is when women are used as political pawns in wars or other violent conflicts. Women's bodies can be used to serve as vehicles for men to express their hatred of and dominance over each other. When a woman functions as a symbol of the potency of the man she belongs to, treating her as a spoil of war means the harm of her rape is not directed primarily toward the woman herself but instead toward the man who owns her. This model also explains why women were raped under chattel slavery: the violence served both as an assertion of a slave owner's power and as a means of emasculating enslaved men who were denied both exclusive sexual access to enslaved women and the ability to protect them.

By insisting that rape is fundamentally a political act, Brownmiller's point is that the meaning of every individual instance of rape cannot be understood unless we look at how gendered sexual violence functions in the larger social picture. In a society like ours, where men's dominance over women is already well established, rape is a way of reasserting this dominance. Women are raped not as individuals, but as members of a subordinate class: as inhabitants of Frye's birdcage. Rape serves as a reminder to both perpetrator and victim that one person is in the dominant class and the other is in the subordinate. In this way, the act of rape both echoes and imposes a social order in which women are inferior beings. What it means to be a man, in this social order, is to be someone with virtually limitless power over women's bodies. What it means to be a woman in this social order is to be someone who is subject to that power, unable to fend it off without the protection of others. "Men who commit rape," Brownmiller charges, "have served in effect as frontline masculine shock troops, terrorist guerrillas in the longest sustained battle the world has ever known."[7]

You have to admit—there's nothing quite like reading the classic works of 1970s feminism to get really creeped out by masculinity. What these theorists might've lacked in nuance they made up for with bone-deep conviction. But while Brownmiller might deserve a round of applause for getting us to pay attention to rape's broader social implications, it's probably worth pumping the brakes a bit on her suggestion that men commit rape as a "conscious process of intimidation." It's unrealistic, Cahill insists, to suggest that the explicit intention motivating every act of rape is a desire to keep women as a class from rising up against the social dominance enjoyed by men as a class. Still, Brownmiller might retort, whether these political motivations are intentional or not, this is their effect.

In Brownmiller and the other second-wave feminists who supported her ideas we can see what was perhaps the first distinctively feminist analysis of rape. In shifting the focus from sex to power, this analysis was noteworthy, in large part, for separating rape from the attractiveness and behavior of its victims, and from sexuality in general. If rape is understood to be primarily about power, not sexual attraction, then the focus shifts from a portrait with men painted as lustful brutes barely in control of their natural appetites who are entirely dependent on the civilizing forces of women's natural modesty to one that acknowledges that this all-too-common act of gendered violence is about hierarchy.

This feminist analysis of rape also overturns the common misconception that rape is predominantly a violent act in which a woman is assaulted by a stranger. The archetypal rapist might be a pervy creep lurking in the bushes, but the reality is far more mundane. Most sexual assaults are committed by someone a woman knows—often intimately.* Depictions of rapists as stranger assailants who lie in wait to prey on innocent women often feed into cultural narratives that are racist or xenophobic, when in most cases the dominance being expressed in rape occurs within the context of socially sanctioned relationships. Rape is something that typically happens in marriages or on dates: the hierarchical power that's reinforced by these acts of sexual violence (or the mere threat of them) is the everyday quotidian power that men enjoy over women in a patriarchal society.

One of the key points feminists are making here is that sex should happen in a situation where the conditions are such that consent is freely given and it's a genuine option for it to be revoked at any time. On this way of looking at things, sexual violence is better characterized as the absence of consent, or the absence of conditions for consent. If saying no isn't really a live option then any yes you might give isn't really a meaningful yes, is it? Understood in this way, a lot of heterosexual sex probably isn't entirely consensual, because women don't have the social power that would let them refuse men's sexual demands. This point is often misinterpreted as a hyperbolic claim that feminists think that "all heterosexual sex is rape," and then employed as a sort of reductio ad absurdum to show that feminists are clearly nuts. "I'm not saying that sex must be rape," insists Andrea Dworkin. "What I think is that sex must not put women in a subordinate

---

* Statistics show 8 out of 10 rapes are committed by someone known to the victim. Only 19.5% of rapes are committed by a stranger, while 39% are committed by an acquaintance, 33% by a current or former partner, 6% by more than one person or the victim cannot remember, and 2.5% by a non-spouse relative. Rape, Abuse & Incest National Network, "Perpetrators of Sexual Violence: Statistics," accessed November 11, 2019, https://www.rainn.org/statistics/perpetrators -sexual-violence; *National Crime Victimization Survey, 2010–2016*, Department of Justice, Office of Justice Programs, Bureau of Justice Statistics, 2017.

position. It must be reciprocal and not an act of aggression from a man looking only to satisfy himself."[8]

This feminist understanding of rape as being inherently about power, not sexual desire, is also useful for shedding light on the prevailing tendency to blame the victims of rape in ways we wouldn't dream of blaming the victims of other crimes. Many of us, including those in the court system, continue to imply that women who are sexually harassed or assaulted have brought it on themselves in some way. We do it every time we ask what a woman was doing before the incident occurred. We do it every time we ask what she was wearing, or whether she was drinking, or if she was out alone. We do it every time we ask how many sexual partners she's had, or anything else about her sexual history. We do it every time we suggest that different behavior on her part might have led to a different outcome.

I still remember the first time the absurdity of the thought that women who are subjected to sexual harassment or assault are somehow "asking for it" came crashing down on me. Many years ago, while attending university in a small western Canadian city, I was walking to campus on a forty-below-zero-degree afternoon when a carful of catcalling dudes drove by.[*] As I reflexively moved to flip them the bird, I realized that I was stymied by the enormous puffy mittens obscuring my fingers from view. As a matter of fact, my entire body was shrouded in billowing puffy layers. Virtually no skin could've been exposed, because if it had been it would've been frostbitten within minutes. I was wearing the least sexy outfit imaginable, and yet that still wasn't enough to forestall street harassment. The only

---

[*] Fun fact: Negative forty degrees is where the Celsius and Fahrenheit scales meet! This is useful insofar as it permits me to relay this story without having to do the mental conversion I somehow still have such a hard time with even after all these years as an expat.

thing that marked me out as female was the fact that my scarf happened to be pink.

I knew their behavior wasn't about sexiness. And it sure as hell wasn't meant as a compliment on my sartorial choices—I looked like the Michelin Man. Their catcalling was an assertion of male social dominance: these guys were letting me know (and simultaneously proving to one another) that their social status permitted them to make unsolicited and unwelcome comments on how I as a woman was allowed to move through public space. Short of leaving the house with an invisibility cloak, I had no way to avoid their harassment. And yet too many people still insist that if women just acted differently, then men would behave themselves and that women are the ones responsible for directing men's eyes (and thus their loins) in our direction.

Feminism gives us a different analysis of street harassment. Describing her experience of an incident differing from mine only in its good fortune to take place in considerably more hospitable weather, Sandra Bartky argues:

> While it is true that for these men I am nothing but, let us say, a "nice piece of ass," there is more involved in this encounter than their mere fragmented perception of me. They could, after all, have enjoyed me in silence. Blissfully unaware, breasts bouncing, eyes on the birds in the trees, I could have passed by without having been turned to stone. But I must be *made* to know that I am a "nice piece of ass": I must be made to see myself as they see me.... It is unclear what role is played by sexual arousal or even spontaneous connoisseurship in encounters like these. What I describe seems less the spontaneous expression of a healthy eroticism than a ritual of subjugation.[9]

This behavior isn't just a "way of perceiving," Bartky insists, it's a "way of maintaining dominance."[10]

The idea of "civil inattention," coined by the sociologist Erving Goffman to describe respectful encounters between people who don't know each other, is a useful tool in this context.[11] When we make brief eye contact with a stranger and then avert our eyes as we walk by them, acknowledging that we see them but signaling that we don't intend to invade their personal space, that's civil inattention. The effect of civil inattention, according to Goffman, is a kind of privacy in public that makes anonymous life in urban settings possible. The norm holds for male-only and female-only interactions—but not, as the philosopher Margaret Crouch points out, for all interactions between men and women.[12] Instead, some men treat women as "open persons" who aren't worthy of the social respect that civil inattention is meant to convey. Women can be ogled, stared at, commented on, and approached at will. Understanding such behavior as the breach of a norm whose purpose is to convey respect explains why it's not a compliment, even if it might sometimes masquerade as such.

Rape as Biological Inevitability

While Brownmiller played a key role in bringing attention to sexualized violence as fundamentally a social phenomenon, she still believed that the origin of rape boiled down to an accident of biology. Cis men rape cis women simply because they can:

> Without a biologically determined mating season, a human male can evince sexual interest in a human female at any time he pleases and his psychologic urge is not dependent in the slightest on her biological readiness or receptivity.... Man's structural capacity to rape and

women's corresponding structural vulnerability are as basic to the physiology of both our sexes as the primal act of sex itself.... When men discovered that they could rape, they proceeded to do it.[13]

Brownmiller saw this as a pre-political biological reality: cis men have penises (which can penetrate) and cis women have vaginas (which are penetrable). But feminists who came later would take issue with this characterization of biology as politically neutral. An early articulation of this concern came from philosopher Alison Jaggar, who asserted that "the whole nature/nurture distinction is fundamentally misleading when applied to human beings: we simply cannot identify any social phenomena that are independent of biological influence, nor any human 'natural' or biological features that are independent of social influence."[14] As we saw in chapters 3 and 4, many feminists in Jaggar's wake now reject the sex/gender distinction, instead viewing the sexed body to be as much of a social construction as the gendered one. And if biology isn't politically innocent, then it's a mistake to think that gendered dominance and submission arise naturally from the anatomical possibilities of penetrating and being penetrated. After all, Cahill points out, lots of different parts of our bodies are capable of penetrating and lots of others are capable of being penetrated. Cis women could forcibly penetrate cis men's anuses with their hands, for example, yet they don't. "To view the penis as an instrument of rape," she alleges, "is already to organize the male body in such a way as to privilege the genitals as a grounding of sexuality and to understand heterosexuality as a process of conquest, wherein women are disadvantaged by their inability to use force. Yet under different social and political rubrics, [cis] men do not exist as potential rapists, nor are [cis] women constantly under the threat of rape."[15] Cahill notes that the frequency of rape varies widely across cultures, and in some it is virtually unheard-of. Mere biological possibility doesn't determine what is socially possible, much less socially necessary, nor does it determine the social meaning of what we do with our bodies to others'.

Feminist consensus can be hard to come by, but one bit of it that's emerged from the realization that rape is more about social domination than sexual attraction has been a rejection of overly simplistic biological explanations of gendered sexual violence. Most feminists believe rape springs from culture, not biology, and is thus neither natural nor inevitable. Rape as a gendered phenomenon can't be chalked up to differences in average physical size or strength. It's not like smaller cis men live in fear of being assaulted by larger cis women. Rape is fundamentally a social phenomenon: it's something that men, as men, do to women, as women. Again, this isn't to pretend that cis men are never raped, nor is it to minimize the horrific trauma these men experience. In some cases, it might even be made worse by the fact of the crime cutting against social norms. A man who's been raped also faces emasculation, whereas a woman who's been raped has her femininity (understood as the social recognition of her as a woman) affirmed. But by and large, it is cis men who are doing the raping and it is women (and some men) who are being raped, and this sexualized violence is fundamentally an assertion of masculine social dominance.

Pornography

If rape isn't the result of natural biological urges, then where does it come from? If rape is a social phenomenon, then what are the social mechanisms responsible for creating and sustaining it? Around the same time Brownmiller was blaming biology, another band of radical feminists, led by Catharine MacKinnon and Andrea Dworkin, were laying the blame somewhere else entirely: at the feet of pornography.

> Pornography sexualizes rape, batter[y], sexual harassment, prostitution, and child sexual abuse; it thereby celebrates, promotes, authorizes, and legitimizes them. More generally, it eroticizes the dominance and submission that is the [common] dynamic. It makes hierarchy sexy and calls that "the truth about sex" or just a mirror of reality. Through this process pornography constructs what a woman is as what men want from sex.... What pornography does goes beyond its content: it eroticizes hierarchy, it sexualizes inequality.... Pornography is neither harmless fantasy nor a corrupt and confused misrepresentation of an otherwise natural and healthy sexual situation. It institutionalizes the sexuality of male supremacy, fusing the eroticization of dominance and submission with the social construction of men and women.[16]

MacKinnon claims that heterosexual pornography teaches us that men are (and should be, and should want to be) sexually active and dominant and that women are (and should be, and should want to be) sexually passive and submissive. Men fuck, women get fucked. Our culture, she argues, has eroticized gendered relations of dominance and submission. We've romanticized the idea that these gendered differences in power are central to the heterosexual erotic experience, and pornography is, as it were, the codification of this idea.

And boy oh boy are there differences in our views about men's and women's sexuality. Men are expected to be sex-obsessed—boys will be boys, after all—but if a woman likes sex as much as guys do, there's something wrong with her. Sex-obsessed men are complimented as "studs" or "players." Women who admit to liking sex a lot, on the other hand, are denigrated as "sluts." Until very recently we didn't even have a derogatory word to describe the male equivalent, instead having to resort to calling men we think aren't properly in control of their sexual appetites "male sluts."*

MacKinnon points out that what we find sexy tends to follow carefully prescribed gendered roles. How we're supposed to think of ourselves as erotic beings, who we're supposed to want to relate to sexually and how we're supposed to want to relate to them: all of this typically follows a set of narrowly circumscribed erotic scripts. But these predictably patterned sexual relations aren't rooted in a pre-social biological reality, and they don't come out of nowhere. Instead, pornography is responsible for constructing men's and women's sexuality—and thus their identities more generally—and, to the extent that pornography succeeds in doing so, its harm becomes invisible. This gendered behavior starts to appear to us that this is just how men and women naturally are, instead of it being how they're taught to be.

To be clear: it's not just our sexual preferences that are being constructed here, MacKinnon thought. It's gender itself. What it means to be a man is to be the sort of person who sexually dominates a woman. What it means to be a woman is to be the sort of person who is sexually submissive to a man. Facing unwanted sexual objectification from men is the common denominator shared by all women. It's what defines our gender: to be a woman is to be treated as a sex object. The direction of explanation here is important for MacKinnon: it's not that men are socialized to be dominant and women are socialized to be submissive and that's why men and women aren't equal. Instead, underlying inequalities in power give rise to the gendered differences

---

* This linguistic lacuna seems finally to have been addressed with the recent introduction of "fuckboy" into the vernacular. If egalitarianism in insults counts as progress, I'll take it.

in traits, behaviors, and roles we see in patriarchal societies, including those in the bedroom. "Dominance," in MacKinnon's words, is prior to "difference."[17] The unequal power between men and women comes first and is what explains the differences we end up seeing between them.

The problem with pornography isn't just its role in limiting our sexual imaginations, then. The real problem with pornography is the direct effects it has on men's behavior. "Pornography is the theory," the radical feminist Robin Morgan surmised, "and rape is the practice."[18] Pornography doesn't merely reflect some people's attitudes toward women; it creates them. "Porn conditions male orgasm to female subordination," said MacKinnon. "It tells men what sex means, what a real woman is, and codes them together in a way that is behaviorally reinforcing."[19] Porn, these feminists controversially argued, is thus *causally responsible for rape*. To support this claim, MacKinnon cited empirical psychological studies reporting that exposure to pornography "increases the immediately subsequent willingness of normal men to aggress against women under laboratory conditions." Porn "makes normal men more closely resemble convicted rapists attitudinally," she declared, "although as a group they don't look all that different from them to start with."[20] And if that's the case, in a culture like ours, where heterosexuality is compulsory and gendered roles of dominance and submission are eroticized through the mechanism of pornography, rape is basically inevitable.*

---

* A quick point of clarification: it's important to understand that the primary focus of MacKinnon's analysis of the harms of pornography isn't the individual women who make pornography; it's women in society. A response to MacKinnon's anti-porn position you often hear is that pornography isn't sexist because the industry pays its female stars significantly more than its male stars. This might be true of those at the top of the industry, but it says nothing of the countless other women in these films. And in any case, this quibbling is beside the point. MacKinnon's primary concern is how the products of this industry affect the full society.

In making claims such as these, remember, MacKinnon and Dworkin were frequently misconstrued as making the much stronger claim that all heterosexual sex is rape. But both denied this. Their point, rather, is that pornography creates social conditions where it isn't really possible for women to say no to sex. In a world saturated with pornography such as ours—one where frat boys joke that "'no' means 'yes,' and 'yes' means 'anal,'"[21]—porn has the effect of "silencing" women's refusals, rendering them incapable of saying anything that actually counts as a refusal of consent. Picking up where MacKinnon left off, philosopher of language Rae Langton argues that pornography stymies women's ability to refuse sex both by objectifying them and depicting them as existing "for sex," and by portraying their attempts to say no as integral components of erotic scenes.[22] The result is what Langton calls "illocutionary silencing": "although the appropriate words can be uttered, those utterances fail to count as the actions they were intended to be."[23]

The obvious feminist response to this diagnosis of sexual violence was to go after the mechanism. Teaming up with Dworkin, MacKinnon crafted a legal argument claiming that pornography violates women's rights insofar as it maintains sex as a basis for discrimination, keeping "all women in an inferior status by defining our subordination as our sexuality and equating that with our gender."[24] Because pornography directly contributes to women's inequality, MacKinnon and Dworkin argued, there was a legal basis for censoring it. To those who argued that censoring porn would be a violation of the right to free speech of those who produced and disseminated it, they countered that pornography was itself a kind of speech, one that silenced women's ability to criticize pornographic culture or refuse sex. The feminist legal battle over pornography was thus framed as a competition between pornographers' rights to free speech and women's rights to the same (and not, as conservative critics of pornography would have it, as a competition between free speech rights and anti-obscenity moralism). Using arguments that proposed to treat pornography as a violation of women's civil rights, MacKinnon and Dworkin drafted and helped pass local ordinances restricting access to pornography in cities such as Minneapolis, Minnesota, and Indianapolis, Indiana, but these ordinances were quickly either vetoed by local mayors or overturned as unconstitutional in federal courts. In Canada, however, the Supreme Court passed a ruling in 1992, one that remains active today, that incorporated some elements of this legal approach to pornography into its obscenity law.

The Sex Wars

In the years that followed, a rift developed in the feminist movement between an anti-porn faction that followed MacKinnon and Dworkin in thinking that pornography was at the root of most patriarchal evils, on the one hand, and "pro-sex" or "sex-positive" feminists, on the other hand, who accused anti-porn feminists of sexual puritanism and moral authoritarianism. Led by the feminist writer and activist Ellen Willis, pro-sex feminists argued that MacKinnon's view of sex denied women the right to sexual pleasure and bolstered the "neo-Victorian" belief that sex was something men desired but women merely put up with.[25] The feminist sex wars were on.

Defending the idea that sexual desire was something women had just as much a right to as any man, sex-positive feminists such as Gayle Rubin denounced the unfair cultural restrictions and high costs imposed on women who choose to be sexually active.[26] Others, such as writer Dorothy Allison, founded groups like the New York–based Lesbian Sex Mafia, which dedicated themselves to fostering the uninhibited expression of lesbian sexuality. Good Vibrations, a sex-positive and women-centered alternative to the "adult" bookstores of the day, opened its doors in San Francisco in 1977. *On Our Backs,* the first women-run magazine of erotica by and for lesbians, came out in 1984—its title a satirical takedown of *Off Our Backs,* the long-running radical feminist newspaper that published the work of many anti-porn feminists. While anti-porn feminists might have wanted to write sex-positive feminists off as unthinking and uncritical cheerleaders who'd been deluded into doing the patriarchy's work for it, many sex-positive feminists were in fact early critics of the misogyny and lack of variety in pornography, calling for more woman-made and explicitly feminist porn and speaking out about the many unfair ways in which society constrained women sexually.[27] What bound sex-positive feminists together was a shared assertion of a woman's right to sexual pleasure for its own sake and an insistence on finding ways to understand this pleasure beyond male terms.

Meanwhile, for all their sincere concern about how pornography was harming women, MacKinnon, Dworkin, and their allies showed themselves willing to if not exactly hop into bed with anti-porn conservatives, then to at least not publicly distance themselves from this regressive agenda as vociferously as they should have. (When Phyllis Schlafly goes on the record endorsing your anti-pornography ordinance, there's a serious feminist problem.)* Led by men such as James Dobson, leader of the fundamentalist Christian organization Focus on the Family, and Edwin Meese, the Republican attorney general whose Commission on Pornography recommended tougher laws against porn in the name of diminishing violence against women, these social conservatives took issue with pornography's uncritical

---

* Schlafly endorsed the Indianapolis anti-pornography ordinance in her national newsletter as an inspired means of restricting pornography's reach.

portrayals of extramarital sex and its incitement of lust and mas-
turbation. Decrying a "floodtide of filth" sweeping the nation,
they used their anti-pornography campaigns to lay the ground-
work for the "family values" agenda that would go on to shift
the country to the right after Reagan's 1980 election.[28] Anti-porn
feminists' willingness to make political hay with people like this
should probably give you the willies—it certainly does for me.

Given the explosion of pornography in the decades since the
feminist sex wars, it's safe to say that the pro-sex feminists have
won out—if only because with the advent of the internet it's no
longer an option to censor pornography even if we wanted to.
(MacKinnon and Dworkin were publishing their ideas in the
1980s, when the primary vehicles for porn's dissemination were
magazines, movie theaters, and early VCR cassettes.) But this
anti-porn analysis shouldn't be written off as just some historical relic. As far as I'm concerned, MacKinnon and Dworkin are
used as whipping girls by too many feminist critics who don't
appreciate just how influential and sophisticated their analysis has been. What these critics often fail to realize is that there
are at least three distinct layers to MacKinnon and Dworkin's
argument:

1. A **causal** argument: Viewing pornography, either directly or
   indirectly, causes men to rape women.
2. A **legal** argument: Following from this, pornography should
   be censored or otherwise legislated against because it harms
   women through rape.
3. A **moral** argument: The gendered roles of dominance and
   submission that are represented in pornography are deeply
   morally problematic.

Once you evaluate these arguments separately, it becomes
clear that some of them have **fared better than others**. The

causal argument fails to withstand the scrutiny of empirical analysis. For one thing, if it were accurate (if viewing pornography directly causes men to rape women), then there should've been considerably less sexual violence against women in earlier centuries when porn was less prevalent, and the increased availability of pornography on the internet should have resulted in a dramatic increase in the rate of rape. But sexual assault was already ubiquitous before technology made porn so widely available. And what's more, rape, like all violent crime, has actually decreased since MacKinnon and Dworkin wrote in the 1980s—by some estimates, it's fallen by 49 percent since 1993.[29] Also, some countries (for example, China and many countries in the Middle East) have banned pornography—while it does circulate, it's harder to come by—but their rates of sexual violence against women are, if anything, higher than those in countries that don't censor pornography. Finally, an analogy to violent movies and video games can be made here. These forms of media don't seem to directly cause violence, but they do seem to increase subjective reports of one's willingness to be violent. (Basically, when you walk out of a super-violent action movie, you're much likelier to say that you would kick a bad guy's butt. But there's very little evidence that you'd actually do so if the opportunity presented itself.) Maybe MacKinnon and Dworkin's claims about pornography's effects on "the immediately subsequent willingness of normal men to aggress against women under laboratory conditions" should be understood in a similar way: subjective reports don't always map onto objective reality.

Still, we don't have to assume there's a direct causal link between exposure to pornography and rape (of the form: X watches porn and is immediately inspired to rape Y) to think the two are entangled. And, sure, the answer here almost certainly isn't censorship: given that the US courts have spoken so unambiguously in ruling against the legal tenability of censoring most pornography, the legal argument has virtually no legs to stand on. But this doesn't mean MacKinnon and Dworkin weren't onto something with their moral analysis of pornography.

Even if we admit that there's probably nothing wrong with pornographic imagery *per se*—that there's a deep and healthy human need that's being addressed through sexualized depictions of naked bodies—that doesn't mean that all pornography is morally unproblematic. It really all depends on what *type* of porn we're talking about, and if it's the type of porn that celebrates women being debased, degraded, subordinated, insulted, and violated, then every feminist bone in our bodies should resist.

In her feminist defense of pornography, philosopher Nancy Bauer celebrates the variety in porn—one is reminded of "rule 34" of the internet: if it exists, there is porn of it—for its ability to overcome the alienation people might've felt in the days before the internet allowed us to connect with our fellows in freakiness, no matter how outré. Porn can help us discover that "the twists and turns of [our] erotic longing are not sui generis, that no one is a true sexual freak. Insofar as it substitutes for the psychoanalyst's couch, it can increase our real-world sexual self-awareness."[30] The porn world is a fictional utopia, Bauer says, where the rules of respect and consent are turned on their heads, a world where using "another person solely as a means to satisfy one's own desire is the ultimate way to respect that person's humanity and even humanity in general."[31] This utopia offers an escape from the real world of sexual frustrations, anxieties, incompatibilities, and mediocrities, but no one is seriously pretending that the rules of the porn world should carry over to the real world.

However, the problem with Bauer's defense of pornography is that it gives us no real explanation of why *this particular* utopia has such a draw over us. For all the variety now available, most heterosexual porn is depressingly, and distressingly, the same.

It's horrifically sexist. It celebrates and revels in the violation and debasement of the female body. It glamorizes women's lack of consent. The very setting of most heterosexual porn—where the sexual dimorphism of barely legal women being dominated by older and physically stronger men is eroticized—is one where the conditions for consent are dubious at best. And this isn't the fringe stuff. This is the mainstream material.

The cultural conversation that feminists in MacKinnon and Dworkin's wake are pleading with people to have is as relevant as ever. It's a conversation that keeps uncomfortable questions like these at the forefront: *Why are we, collectively, turned on by men dominating women? What's hot about physically harming women? Why do we get off on controlling, subjugating, and demeaning women? What the hell is wrong with us?*

Sexual Objectification

What's going on, most feminists agree, is informed by our culture's entrenched sexual penchant for treating women like they're pieces of meat. This sexual objectification involves treating a woman as if she were an object—a mere thing to be used for someone else's sexual pleasure. Instead of respecting a woman as a complex autonomous individual with desires and goals, an objectifier treats her as if she were only a body, or even only a fetishized body part. When we sexually objectify a woman we use her, or ignore her wishes, or treat her as if what she's experiencing doesn't matter, which is precisely what's often happening in sexual harassment and assault, in pornography, and in many of popular culture's portrayals of women in general. As comic-book writer Kelly Sue DeConnick bemoans, in way too many books and movies the female characters could be replaced with sexy lamps without the plot being affected in the slightest.[32]

Unlike sexy lamps, real women have thoughts and dreams

and goals and ambitions and desires of their own. But all these inconveniences can be ignored when a woman is objectified. Philosopher Linda LeMoncheck argues that objectification amounts to a form of dehumanization, which undermines women's equal moral status, resulting in their being treated as if they have fewer rights to well-being and freedom than the men who objectify them.[33] When women are viewed as if their primary function is men's sexual gratification, women's goals, interests, and preferences are inevitably granted less importance than those of their objectifiers. Women are, in effect, thereby granted a second-class moral status. Because the way women are viewed affects the way they're treated, and the way they're treated affects the way they're viewed, women's sexual objectification both derives from and contributes to women's oppression in general.

Of course, it's important not to confuse treating women as sex objects, which is by definition morally problematic, with treating them as sexually attractive or as the objects of sexual desire, which can be fine.[34] There's a concern that some feminist criticism of the sexual objectification in heterosexual porn risks papering over the reality that objectification can be arousing, and that women also sexually objectify men at times. "Not always, not under every circumstance, not for every person in every situation," admits Bauer. "But everyone is sometimes sexually aroused by the objectification of a person or people whose humanity is, at that moment, beside the point. This experience is not unique to porn consumers: every normal adult is familiar with that twinge of desire that a stranger, real or depicted, can instantly evoke."[35]

But no feminist is realistically saying that you mustn't ever look at a woman with lust. No one is saying you can't treat a woman as if her body, or even just certain particularly sexy parts of her body, are the most important things about her at any given moment. We're just saying you should reserve this sexual gaze and treatment for situations where it's appropriate—like, *when you're actually having consensual sex with her.* The morally dicey kind of sexual objectification occurs when a woman is treated as sexually attractive or available in a context where her sexuality ought to be irrelevant, or when it's used as a way to fail to treat her as an equal because of her sex. When they're sexually objectified in these ways, women are treated as if their subjectivity and autonomy—their feelings and experiences, and their decisions about what they want to do or how they want to be treated—don't matter.

Internalized Objectification

As we saw in chapter 2's discussion of internalized oppression, this objectification isn't just something that's imposed upon women from without. When women internalize the message that our worth stems from how sexually appealing we are to men— and given the prevalence of this message, it's almost impossible to completely avoid absorbing it—we end up objectifying ourselves. And so we become our own panoptical jailers, taking on the work of seeing ourselves from the point of view of the men who desire us. Knowing that our life prospects will likely depend on how we are appraised by the male connoisseur, we learn to appraise ourselves first and best.

Simone de Beauvoir says this situation disposes us toward seeing our bodies not as instruments to be harnessed in the service of our own life projects but as objects destined for the purposes of another. We escape into the narcissistic pleasures of the mirror to avoid taking responsibility for our lives. Along with most other existentialists, de Beauvoir knew how terrifying living an existentially authentic life can be. Given the opportunity, most people will do anything to avoid taking on the burden of deciding for ourselves what our lives will be about, even though making self-defining choices is what existentialists think is the very thing that makes us human.* We'd rather follow the herd, rather latch on to someone else's stories about what is meaningful, rather fall in line with what's expected of us by social convention than buck up and face the reality that each of us is alone in this world and the only meaning that exists is that we make for ourselves. Women aren't uniquely cowardly in this regard, but our gender roles do provide us with distinctively feminine opportunities to avoid the challenges of existential freedom. Indulging in the self-absorbed pleasures of feminine self-objectification, for de Beauvoir, is a matter of falling prey to the temptations of existential inauthenticity. We do so if we allow ourselves to be objects for men, to let them define us, rather than face the arduous work of being subjects who must decide for ourselves what will define our lives. It's easier, less scary, to help ourselves to the small delights of feminine vanity available to us if we follow traditional social scripts than it is to buck convention and do the hard work of living an existentially authentic existence.

Building on de Beauvoir's analysis, Bartky argues that there's more going on in women's self-objectification than just an attempt to avoid the terrors of existential responsibility. It's not merely from the point of view of an internalized male gaze that women evaluate themselves, but from that of an internalized representative of what she calls the "fashion-beauty complex." "Like the 'military-industrial complex,' the fashion-beauty

---

* A dog doesn't lie awake at night torturing himself about whether he's a bad boy because he peed on the rug. A rat doesn't ask herself whether she wants to be the kind of rat who runs through mazes for cheese. These animals just are what they are, and they can't be otherwise. We humans, on the other hand, decide for ourselves what sorts of creatures we're going to be. "Existence precedes essence," existentialists famously say. This means that we decide for ourselves what our essences will be. But existentialists know full well how difficult—how scary—it can be to have to make decisions as big as this.

complex is a major articulation of capitalist patriarchy," Bartky explains. "Overtly, the fashion-beauty complex seeks to glorify the female body and to provide opportunities for narcissistic indulgence. More important than this is its *covert* aim, which is to depreciate [a] woman's body and deal a blow to her narcissism."[36] By feeding us an endless stream of impossible images of feminine beauty, the industry has figured out how to garner immense profit from simultaneously creating and then placating women's narcissistic insecurities. Women internalize their status as sex objects, then, because a lot of people who are very good at making money have a great deal invested in encouraging us to do so.

Feminists are getting better at acknowledging the importance of keeping intersectional concerns at the forefront of the analysis of sexual objectification. We've seen the dangers that lurk when we go looking for the set of characteristics or experiences that are supposed to be shared in common by all women; anytime a feminist claims to have identified the one thing that binds all women together, the hairs on the back of your neck should be standing up. Some feminists have thus criticized MacKinnon's view that sexual objectification is the thing that makes women into women for failing to take into account the ways that women's experience of their sexuality is affected by factors such as race and class.[37] During slavery, for example, while white women were thought of as sexually virtuous and pure, black women were hypersexualized and viewed as always sexually available—so much so that the rape of a black woman was thought to be impossible.[38] These racist beliefs might be less explicit today, but they persist, showing themselves, for example, in a news cycle that obsesses over the assault or abduction of white girls and women while often ignoring these crimes when they're visited on girls and women of color. How sexual objectification affects women's lives also varies drastically according to class privilege: a wealthy woman might get to sign up for the perks of a being a trophy wife, an upper-middle-class woman might have the luxury of not needing to rely heavily on her looks to get ahead in her career while a lower-middle-class woman might have no choice but to do so, and a poor woman might work in the sex industry, even though she'd really rather not, because it's her best financial option for survival. What sexual objectification looks like is vastly different depending on your life circumstances. Even internalized objectification—when women take on the work of turning ourselves into objects for male consumption—will mean something very different for a woman whose able-bodied cis whiteness makes her a paradigm of feminine beauty than it will for a woman who is disabled, or trans, or of color.

Toxic Masculinity

Of course, women aren't the only ones who internalize their roles in this mess. Nor are we the only ones harmed by these roles. I hate to burst the bubble of those men's rights activists who portray feminists as man-hating harpies, but we're not the ones who say this is inevitable. We're not the ones who think that men are fundamentally lustful, mouth-breathing brutes who are incapable of controlling themselves, who but for the civilizing strictures of polite society would be running around humping anything vaguely vagina-shaped. Instead, we think most men are fundamentally decent creatures who've been sold a bad bill of goods about what's expected of them and what they're entitled to in return.

The term "toxic masculinity" is at risk of being beaten to death these days, but there's truth behind the phrase nevertheless: our culture's ideas about what it means to be a man are deeply messed up. Men are expected to be emotionally stunted, unflaggingly stoic, and willing to work themselves into an early grave in order to support a family. In return, they're told they can expect to receive a certain set of entitlements: an implicit ownership of public space they're free to manspread over, the authority to manterrupt and mansplain the terms of every conversation, and, most important for our purposes here, the right to women's sexual attention and compliance—*mentitlement*, according to the latest of these portmanteaus.

Masculine loathing of women runs deep in our culture. Some gay men express this loathing by boasting of their "platinum star" status—earned by not only having never had sex with someone of the opposite sex (which makes you a "gold star" in the queer community), but also by having been born by cesarean section (thus having avoided any contact whatsoever with a repulsive vagina). But misogyny doesn't always manifest as overt hatred. Philosopher Kate Manne argues that misogyny is often better understood as applying to social systems as a whole, where women face hostility "because they are women in a man's world (i.e., a patriarchy)."[39] In this guise, misogyny actually manifests as approval as long as women conform to the feminine roles expected of them. It's only when women violate gendered expectations or intrude on what has traditionally been seen as the province of men that misogyny turns into a desire to put them back in their place.

Men who buy into mentitlement view sex and companionship from women as the expected, almost contractual, reward for good behavior. As long as women are appropriately subordinate to them, these men respond with kindness and respect. But as soon as women stop giving them what they expect, these men react with hostility and anger. If they're Nice Guys, they merely complain about being friend-zoned (never mind that they had no right to the woman's sexual attention in the first place). If they're less nice, it can get a lot uglier than that. Just dip your toe into the online communities of "incels"—"involuntary celibates" who blame their inability to have sex on women's shallowness instead of the misogynist repugnance of their worldview.[40]

I'm not sure most cis men really understand what it's like to spend your life in dread that a man might decide he wants you when you don't want him. Guarding yourself against that possibility structures too many aspects of your public persona. It can inform your decisions about how to dress, how to speak, how to carry yourself, how much eye contact to make, and how friendly to be. But no matter the situation, no matter your credentials, no matter how carefully you guard your behavior, no matter how hard you've worked, no matter how completely irrelevant sex is (or should be) to the situation, a man still might decide that he thinks you're hot. And then it's your problem. It's up to you to do something about it. You get a sinking feeling in the pit of your stomach. Oh God, not this again. He's careful to protect himself with a veneer of plausible deniability, secure in the knowledge that people will believe him if he needs to write you off as crazy if things go south and you try to call him out on what's going on. He's the one who sets the terms of the encounter, but it's up to you to deal with the situation. He gets to sniff you like a dog after food, still you're responsible for dealing with his appetites.

And yet you might find yourself experiencing a twinge of pride. A sense of accomplishment: success at femininity! You've been told overtly or covertly your whole life that your purpose in life is to be appealing to men. You've been trained to crave men's approval, and now there's this tiny kernel of affirmation.* Of course you feel this way. You've spent your life being groomed

---

* And my but we're hungry for it, aren't we ladies? (This is captured brilliantly, and hilariously, in *Crazy Ex-Girlfriend*'s "Love Kernels" sketch. Rachel Bloom, "Love Kernels," *Crazy Ex-Girlfriend,* YouTube video, October 24, 2016, accessed November 11, 2019, https://www.youtube.com/watch?v=bkAjUBtn_TM.)

by and for the heteropatriarchy. But often then your feeling turns back to disgust, now also with yourself for craving this approval you know is ultimately degrading for you. Maybe there's an extra iteration or two of this loop, informed by your experiences as a woman who's used to being told you don't meet society's standards of sexual attractiveness because you're poor or disabled or black or brown or trans. You still end up at the same spot: stuck dealing with a man's desires that you do not share.

The real kicker is that it's up to women to make this dance OK. And we do. We are so good at making nice that we usually don't even notice we're doing it. We are so damned good at our jobs that we've managed to make everyone—ourselves especially—forget how much work we're doing. We dodge the drunken pawing, we laugh off the awkward innuendo, we meekly apologize for friend-zoning the guy, we pretend he isn't flirting with us, we bend over backwards to avoid making men feel bad about themselves.

The only time anyone ever notices that something is amiss is when women can't, or won't, keep doing the work of smoothing things over. This, to my mind, is the real significance of the MeToo movement: suddenly, the cat's out of the bag. We hit a tipping point and the accretion of male sins finally became impossible to ignore. And now so many of us have been able to tell our stories. MeToo has laid bare our culture's eroticized gendered relationships of dominance and submission.

CHAPTER 6

WHERE THE RUBBER MEETS THE ROAD

Consciousness-raising—coming to recognize that you and others like you are stuck in a birdcage—can be eye-opening, even empowering. But let's be honest: it can also be super depressing. Once you start down the feminist rabbit hole you can't unknow what you've learned, and life can start to feel a bit hopeless. The feminist theorist Judith Lorber said that for most people talking about gender is a bit like fish talking about water—when something is so pervasive that it structures virtually every interaction you have with other people, it can be hard to notice, much less consider the possibility that things could be otherwise.[1] Once you start to realize that you live in world of blinkered and limiting social opportunity, of potential harassment and rape, despair and paralysis can be reasonable responses.

I get it. No one wants to read a book that only relentlessly beats them over the head about how broken the world is. So in this last chapter, I want to give you some practical steps for escaping or at least shaking the crap out of the birdcage.

First, know your enemy. As I hope I've shown, men, in general, are not the enemy. They, too, are shaped in a patriarchal system that creates their assumptions about men and women.

Men can be co-opted by a culture that plays on their insecurities or promises to entrench the tacit benefits they glean from a sexist culture. They can be lured into thinking they're superior to women in an attempt to make up for the stings of racism and classism. They can fail to be properly critical of our culture's narratives about what they're entitled to. But men, in general, are as much at the mercy of patriarchy's whims as any woman.

Feminism's real enemies are those men and women who willingly support a patriarchal society and its social institutions, norms, assumptions, and expectations that function below the level of which we're usually consciously aware. Sexism is effective and ubiquitous and pernicious enough that it sometimes might feel like a conspiracy hatched by a bunch of old white dudes in an oak-paneled boardroom somewhere, but I assure you that no feminists think sexism works this way. It'd be easier, honestly, if we could just identify a few (or a whole cart of) bad sexist apples and haul them off to reeducation camps or whatever. But because sexism probably goes back to the beginnings of human civilization and often functions below the level of conscious awareness, getting rid of patriarchy is going to require more than culling the herd. We need to strategize for the long game.

We've already come across some concrete things you can do in previous chapters: Quit with the gender-reveal parties and start asking why we're so obsessively focused on babies' genitals. Remember that women are brown, black, white, cis, trans, queer, straight, rich, poor, and differently abled. Stop thinking that a feminism crafted by corporations hawking fantasies of female empowerment through body wash is going to do anything to overturn the sexist status quo. Don't judge other women for how they bargain with the patriarchy and start admitting that we're all fallible and just trying to get by—in a world that's as unjust as ours it's inevitable that some actions will entrench sexism. Don't write off a woman as irrational because she's angry or strident (especially if she's a woman of color)—consider the possibility that she's tracking reality, that her anger is precisely the right response.

The time to merely lean in is over. We're done playing nice. After decades of backsliding and backlash we're seeing glimmers of progress on some fronts with the MeToo movement, whose astonishing momentum has opened up new possibilities for political action rooted in the recognition of shared experiences, shared frustrations, and shared ultimatums. Women are starting to band together again, and we're showing ourselves to be a force.

This Won't Be Easy

Still, no one is pretending this change is going to be easy.

Given the systemic nature of what we're up against, individual actions, while good and necessary, can only make a limited difference. Marilyn Frye argues that a hallmark of oppression is being put in situations where you're damned if you do, damned if you don't. Women face a choice between being called a slut if we want to have sex or frigid if we don't. We face a choice between being forced to smile all the time or being told we have resting bitch face. We face a choice between being seen as evil deceivers if we pass as cis or make-believers if we're open about being trans. We face a choice between being called selfish mothers if we want to keep our careers when we have kids or unproductive leeches if we want to be stay-at-home moms. We face a choice between having our needs ignored if we live up to the stereotype of the strong black woman or being seen as weak if we reject this stereotype. We face a choice between being labeled irrational and hormonal if we express our emotions or cold and unfeminine if we don't.

Double binds—situations where there's nothing you can do to successfully navigate a situation—typify women's existence in a patriarchal society because oppression is an overarching system made up of patterns of subordination. This, remember, is why the proper level of analysis for feminism is a macroscopic viewpoint that keeps all the wires of the birdcage in view, one whose force is lost at a level of analysis that refuses to acknowledge the existence of and interconnections between the other wires. It's why, despite the stereotypes, feminists aren't generally in the business of judging or shaming individual women for their actions— we're far more interested in the bigger picture. But it's also why it can be hard to come up with practical strategies for what to do in oppressive circumstances: because a lot of the time it's just a matter of choosing among options that all are pretty dicey.

Sexist oppression also takes so many different forms— especially given the realities of intersectionality—that there isn't a lot of one-size-fits-all advice to be dispensed, the sort that would work for all women in all situations. We've seen how considerations of race, class, sexual orientation, and ability can make for drastically different experiences of what it's like to be a woman. It'd be foolish to expect there to be a lot of concrete guidance that's supposed to work for, or even be relevant to, every woman in every circumstance.

Practical advice can also be thin on the ground because, as anyone with a basic working knowledge of the history of the labor movement can tell you, fighting injustices of the scope we're talking about generally takes collective action. But women's different life experiences make feminist solidarity difficult. We often have more in common with the men in our lives who share our race or class than we do with women across race and class lines.

In 1869, John Stuart Mill saw this lack of solidarity as no accident. He recognized that it serves the patriarchy to keep women divided:

> All causes, social and natural, combine to make it unlikely
> that women should be collectively rebellious to the power

of men. They are so far in a position different from all other subject classes, that their masters require something more from them than actual service. Men do not want solely the obedience of women, they want their sentiments. All men, except the most brutish, desire to have, in the woman most nearly connected with them, not a forced slave but a willing one, not a slave merely, but a favourite. They have therefore put everything in practice to enslave their minds.[2]

Other oppressed groups are at least granted the luxury of hating their oppressors. Women aren't even allowed to recognize our servitude. Instead, we're told that subservience to men is written into our very natures.

All women are brought up from the very earliest years in the belief that their ideal of character is the very opposite to that of men; not self-will, and government by self-control, but submission, and yielding to the control of others. All the moralities tell them that it is the duty of women, and all the current sentimentalities that it is their nature, to live for others; to make complete abnegation of themselves, and to have no life but in their affections. And by their affections are meant the only ones they are allowed to have—those to the men with whom they are connected, or to the children who constitute an additional and indefeasible tie between them and a man.[3]

Mill recognized that women are taught in a whole host of ways that our primary allegiances should be to the men in our lives. We are taught the lesson when we're given our father's surname at birth. We are taught the lesson when our self-worth is tied to whether or not we're sexually appealing to men. We are taught the lesson when we're trained in the skills we'll need to serve our husbands and babies—all those toy kitchens and baby dolls. We are taught the lesson when femininity is less cultur- ally valued than masculinity. ("Fashion," quips author Ruth Whippman, "is vain and shallow, while baseball is basically a branch of philosophy.")[4]

Given all this, is it any wonder that women don't band together more often? It's true that members of other oppressed groups are groomed to accept their subordinate positions in similar ways—there's always something about the nature of a group that justifies its marginalized status—but this grooming doesn't pre- vent solidarity in the same ways because its purpose isn't to tie them to their oppressors.

As de Beauvoir lamented,

> women lack concrete means for organising themselves into a unit which can stand face to face with the correlative unit. They have no past, no history, no religion of their own; and they have no such solidarity of work and interest as that of the proletariat. They are not even promiscuously herded together in the way that creates community feeling among the American Negroes, the ghetto Jews, the workers of Saint-Denis, or the factory hands of Renault.... [W]oman cannot even dream of exterminating the males. The bond that unites her to her oppressors is not comparable to any other. The division of the sexes is a biological fact, not an event in human history.... The couple is a fundamental unity with its two halves riveted together, and the cleavage of society along the line of sex is impossible.[5]

Women can't rise up against men because we need them for financial support, and material protection, and as a means of reproducing. And, less cynically, many of us also happen to love them.

The difficulties of female solidarity, de Beauvoir realized, also exist because we're trained to view one another as the enemy. Heterosexual love pits women against other women, she argued, preventing the possibility of real friendship or solidarity, because other women are viewed primarily as competition. Remember that de Beauvoir thought most women would rather allow ourselves to be defined in terms of what men want from us than face the existential terror of deciding for ourselves what our lives will be about. We fasten onto men's life projects, and these projects become our own. We fasten onto their identities, and these identities become who we are. The threat of losing our male beloved is horrifying, then, because it's tantamount to the threat of losing ourselves. Jealousy directed toward other women is thus an inevitable outcome. "Her entire destiny is involved in each glance her lover casts at another woman, since she has identified her whole being with him," de Beauvoir claims. "Thus she is annoyed if his eyes are turned for an instant toward a stranger; but if he reminds her that she has just been contemplating some stranger, she firmly replies, 'That is not the same thing at all.' She is right."[6] A cuckolded man has had his property defiled or stolen, but a cuckolded woman risks losing something infinitely more valuable.

Straight women's unassailable ties to the men in their lives make the premise of Aristophanes's ancient Greek comedy *Lysistrata* as absurdly comical to us now as it was almost 2,500 years ago. Every once in a while a group of women incorporates the withholding strategy into a larger attempt to gain men's cooperation by refusing to perform the domestic labor that's been assigned to women. Men do tend to take notice when they're sexually frustrated and no one is cooking, or cleaning, or taking care of the kids. Iroquois women tried it in 1600; Icelandic women in 1975; Colombian women in 1997, 2006, and 2011; Liberian women in 2003; Kenyan women in 2009. Some anthropologists even speculate that collective action of this kind played a role in organizing the earliest human societies, explaining the rise of language, culture, and religion. But the long-term effects of these efforts are often negligible. We're too tied to the men in our lives, too much in love with or dependent on fathers and husbands, too protective of brothers and sons, to let ourselves play hardball. Collective action works only if most people are disinclined to or disincentivized from crossing the picket line, and there are often just too many reasons—both practical and emotional—for women to cross to the other side.

Despite these obstacles, women throughout history have successfully managed to come together for all sorts of collective action—from the suffragettes to the ERA to consciousness-raising sessions to anti-rape marches, pro-choice marches, and, most recently, the Women's March. Women have banded together to create domestic-abuse shelters, rape-crisis hotlines, women's lecture series, women's art and film and music festivals, organizations that collect and distribute business attire or menstrual products for women who can't afford them, organizations that help more women get elected to public office, organizations that protect women's reproductive rights, and more. That solidarity among women is difficult doesn't mean it's impossible; history has shown us that. The sisterhood might not ever band together to topple the heteropatriarchal world order in the way other oppressed groups have, but we're still a force to be reckoned with.

And in the meantime, there are some practical feminist strategies to be had for individual women navigating the birdcage. Remember that it's a fool's errand to expect any of this advice to work for, or even apply to, each and every woman in each and every situation. So choose your own adventure. You might find other women at stopping points and join together.

How to Talk About Sex

The ubiquity of sexual violence in our rape culture sets the backdrop against which virtually all sexual encounters take place. It's not a sexy thought, I know. We might wish it weren't so, but pretending otherwise won't make it go away, it'll just make it more likely that we fail to notice these harms or inadvertently worsen them. Thankfully, feminists have given us a ton of tools we can use, both in and out of the bedroom.

CONSENT

Feminist responses to the harms of sexual harassment and violence have, for good reason, tended to focus on the importance of consent. Canadian campus feminists popularized the slogan "No Means No" as part of influential sexual-assault-awareness campaigns that began in the early 1990s. The phrase trickled into American public consciousness as well. The acceptance of "No Means No" into mainstream public discourse marked an important cultural moment, particularly as it helped draw attention to the unwritten rules of sex that eroticize female struggle or refusal, and moved acquaintance rape from the personal to the political realm. But the problem with this negative consent is that it puts the onus on women to resist or refuse sex and it sends the message that any sexual act is OK until a woman says no.

Around the same time that negative consent was getting some cultural uptake, a far more controversial conception of consent was being floated. In 1990, Antioch College introduced the notion of "affirmative consent" in its "Sexual Offense Prevention Policy," an on-campus code of conduct that required consent to be verbally requested and verbally given for each and every step in a sexual encounter. Under the paradigm of affirmative consent, you're not presumed to have said yes unless you

explicitly say no; instead, you're presumed to want to preserve
the boundaries of the most private parts of your body until you
explicitly communicate otherwise. When it comes to something
as personal and intimate as sex, the expectation that people will
keep their hands to themselves until they're explicitly invited to
do otherwise shouldn't strike us as strange, but Antioch's policy ignited a firestorm of public mockery and criticism. It was
widely parodied, perhaps most memorably in a *Saturday Night
Live* skit that depicted the world's least steamy hookups between
robotic students exchanging cringe-worthy questions like "May
I kiss you on the mouth?" and "May I elevate the level of sexual
intimacy by touching your buttocks?" Critics portrayed the policy as the apotheosis of a culture of political correctness bent on
making sex as sterile and unsexy as possible.

But what might have struck many at the time as precious or
sheltered or unrealistic looks now, in the age of MeToo, more
like an approach to sex that was decades ahead of its time. The
students at Antioch realized that these are conversations about
sex that we need to be having. The policy remains in place today,
and its defenders claim that when you formally entrench affirmative consent it fosters a sexual culture that encourages open
communication, honesty, respect, and a lot of exploration and
fun. The community expectations at Antioch are that you've
thought enough about your sexual desires to be able to communicate them to others, and that sex is something you talk
about—before, during, and after—so that the people involved
in the act actually want what's going down to be going down.
Living subject to these norms, apparently, often ends up being
less about policing the desires of others than about owning up
to your own. "It can be really hard to say yes," admits Bethany Saltman, one of the original authors of Antioch's policy.
"You have to be so brazenly wanting sex to say yes." In a world
where women aren't supposed to be avid for sex, to be able to

say: "Yes, I want you to do that to me! Yes, I want to do that to you!" is liberating, she argues, "and that has been totally, totally misunderstood."[7]

Critics want to portray consent-focused models of sexual interaction as the frigid province of uptight prudes, but those who actually use these models know how sexy and liberating it can be. Rebranding consent in sexier terms has been an important feminist step in enabling women to take control of their sexuality. In more recent years, we've seen the rise of a model of "enthusiastic consent." Its proponents think moving away from "No means no" to "Yes means yes" is the path to "a world where women enjoy sex on their own terms and aren't shamed for it, . . . a world where men treat their sexual partners as collaborators, not conquests, . . . a world where rape is rare and punished swiftly."[8] Affirmative consent was written into California law in 2014. "Yes means yes" is now the state's consent standard on college and high school campuses, preventative education is required during student orientations, and increased access to counseling resources and training for adjudication panels is mandated.

Norms of affirmative and enthusiastic consent have long held sway in kink and BDSM scenes, where people obviously have very good reason to want to make sure of consent for each action, and they've begun to take hold in alternative communities such as those at Burning Man. There, the Bureau of Erotic Discourse works to foster a climate of safety and respect for all with "consent propaganda" and training events that remind attendees of chestnuts like that impaired people cannot give consent, that silence is not consent, that consent can be revoked at any time, and that consent for one thing isn't consent for another. At Burning Man's sex parties, organizers kick off the events with exercises like requiring everyone in attendance to request a sexual interaction from a stranger who has been instructed to decline. In an expression of appreciation for setting a boundary, the stranger is then to be thanked for their refusal. Exercises like this might sound staged and forced, but by all accounts making it easier to say no makes all the subsequent yeses even more exciting. Normalizing refusal and thanking people for setting boundaries without explanation or apology set the stage for new, healthier kinds of sexual encounters. When saying no isn't a big deal, it opens up the psychological space to own your desires and to be honest with yourself about what you really want. It also ensures that you're doing things because you want to be doing them, not because you think you're supposed to.

And yet plenty of people still think that affirmative consent has to look like that old *SNL* skit. Nowhere is it written that this communication needs to be awkward or stilted or robotic or legalistic. (Unless you happen to be into that sort of thing, in which case have at it.) "You good?" or "Is this OK?" or "Can I take this [piece of clothing] off?" or "Can I touch you here?" or "How're you doing?" or "Do you like this?" or "Tell me if this is too much, OK?" are all ways of checking in that, said in the right voice and with the right twinkle in your eye, can keep a sexual encounter sexy.

The resilience of the thought that we shouldn't be talking to each other when we're having sex suggests that it's more than shyness or the inherently potentially embarrassing nature of a topic so intimate that's motivating our collective silence. It's also, I suspect, that we've so deeply internalized the belief that sex is wrong, dirty, and shameful that we're often not willing to admit to ourselves (much less to our partners) what we want and what we're doing—even when we're actually doing it. There's also a gendered dynamic here: women aren't supposed to admit that they want sex, much less tell their male partners that they want something different; men are either supposed to ascertain ex nihilo what their female partners want, or just not care.

BEYOND CONSENT

As important and necessary as all this feminist work on consent has been, philosopher Quill Kukla, writing as Rebecca Kukla, thinks the standard model of a request that's followed by consent or refusal isn't how things typically, much less ideally, work in real sexual life.[9] A better way to think about sexual negotiation, they say, takes *invitations,* rather than requests, as paradigmatic. "I was wondering if you'd like to come up to my hotel room with me?" isn't a request you consent to, it's an invitation you accept or turn down. Invitations differ from requests in a number of ways: they're governed by complex norms of hospitality that are sensitive to power dynamics; they can be rude or inappropriate if offered in the wrong context; they make invitees feel welcome but not obliged; and, quirkily, they call for gratitude from both the inviter and invitee if accepted. You thank me for coming up to your room, I thank you for asking me.

Sexual communication doesn't stop once we've decided that we want to have sex. Ideally, we communicate what we like, what's on and off the table, whether and how much we're enjoying ourselves, what we might want to try, how much we're appreciating our partner(s), whether we want to change tracks, when we want to stop, and so on. A unique and particularly important tool for ethical sexual communication, says Kukla, is the practice of employing *safe words*. Whether it's a random word that wouldn't ordinarily come up in normal sexual conversation (like "kimchi"), an unambiguous phrase that's not open to misinterpretation (like "safe word"), or a coded system that allows for a bit more nuance (like "green"/"yellow"/"red"), safe words are negotiated beforehand and allow partners to communicate to each other in no uncertain terms when they want a sexual activity to end. It's pretty simple, really: when the safe word is uttered, playtime is over (or modified in a pre-agreed-upon way). Not surprisingly, safe words originated in the BDSM community, where folks were incentivized to figure out how to fulfill sexual desires that would be dangerous to attempt without clear safety procedures. Kukla thinks we'd do well to unleash safe words on the bedrooms of the world. It'd be fantastic, they say, were instruction in their use to be a standard protocol in sex education for teenagers. Safe words give sex partners an unambiguous way to stop sex acts without having to give a reason or explanation—important for anyone interested in testing their limits, but especially valuable for young people who are just beginning to figure out what they want. Safe words also give people a way to explore their sexual interests while ensuring that their partner's limits are heard and respected.

How to Talk to Kids

OK, now that you've been armed with a better sense of how to talk to other grown-ups, we can move on to smaller fry.

What's the first thing you do when you're making small talk with a little girl? You compliment her on her dress. You comment on her hair. You tell her she's looking pretty today. You call her "princess." How do you make small talk with little boys? You surely don't comment on what they look like or what they're wearing. You ask them what they like to do, whether they like soccer or dinosaurs or rocket ships or bugs. Start doing the same with girls. Girls beam when you call them pretty because they've learned that it's the highest compliment our culture has for them, but you can help them to start unlearning it. Ask them what they like to read. Ask them what they like to do. Talk to them about literally anything other than their external appearance. It might be hard to do at first. Notice what that says about how much you've internalized gendered expectations.

The birdcage isn't going to be dismantled unless we start

noticing and identifying each and every single one of its wires. These conversational tropes might seem harmless or insignificant, but when we take part in them we're basically acting as the shock troops for the sexist enculturation of women. We're communicating to girls, in no uncertain terms, that what is expected of them is that they be visually pleasing (to men), and that what counts as visually pleasing is a very narrowly circumscribed performance of cis white femininity that is historically defined by cis white men's interests. We're grooming girls to hinge their self-worth on their sexual desirability to men, and if all this isn't starting to feel a little creepy and pervy to you by now, then you're not paying attention.

It's probably worth mentioning that this isn't just an issue that concerns our daughters. We need to change the ways we talk to boys too. Try talking to them about their appearance once in a while. Tell them how pretty they're looking. Compliment them on their clothing and haircuts. Try to get the message across that being stylish and nice to look at isn't a bad thing. Notice how hard it is to do all this too.

In many ways, we police gender-nonconformity in boys far more rigidly than we do in girls. Girls have been able to wear pants for generations now, but boys in skirts remain decidedly out of the ordinary. You can now find the occasional progressive bubble where people are happy to let boys come to school in princess dresses, but these pockets are the exception not the rule. More often, boys face far fewer options for gender expression than girls. Many parents are relatively content to have a daughter who's a tomboy—some even encourage it, believing that a girl who's athletic or strong-willed or assertive will be set up to do better in life in our hypercompetitive culture. But most parents censor activities, language, or dress in boys if they seem feminine. Meanwhile, toy manufacturers have been happy to develop new lines of toys for girls that were traditionally meant for boys—So. Much. Pink. LEGO.—but makeup and princess dresses for boys aren't exactly flying off the shelves. We see this disparity in children's literature as well, where even as we're starting to see more tales of bold and adventurous girls, books about boys enjoying cooking or babysitting or fashion remain pretty much nonexistent. The reason girls are afforded a bit more flexibility in their gender performances than boys is because we valorize masculinity and denigrate femininity.

Our social rejection of feminine boys isn't just about the mutually reinforcing connections between sexism and homophobia (although it's partly about that, to be clear). It's also because a boy drawn to feminine interests threatens to upset the value system that undergirds the status quo. No wonder they're looked upon with distress. Masculinity is synonymous with power, so it's less surprising and disturbing when girls try to seize it than when a boy willingly takes on undervalued feminine interests and traits. Such a boy's actions suggest that we're wrong in our value judgments, which threatens societal norms and explains the lengths we'll go—social ostracism, harassment, violence—to disabuse him of his proclivities.

The trans feminist author Julia Serano describes a childhood in which, "as a somewhat eccentric kid, I was given plenty of leeway to opt out of boys' activities and to cultivate an androgynous appearance and persona. I was sometimes teased for being different, for being an atypical or unmasculine boy, but it was nothing compared to the venom that was reserved for those boys who acted downright feminine."[10] Serano, we saw, argues that the hostility experienced by trans women, who "willingly" forego the perks of masculinity that are supposed to be their birthright, is often less a matter of transphobia than it is of misogyny.

How to Deal with a Manspreader

The double binds of sexist oppression can make strategies for dealing with men behaving badly in public spaces pretty scarce. When it comes to street harassment, for instance, it can feel like there are no satisfying ways to respond to a catcaller: if you ignore the guy then you affirm the stereotype of women as docile and afraid, but any response you give him will likely affirm his ability to get your goat. Still, in my experience, there are things you can do. You can call BS on a harasser's pretense that his catcalls are merely compliments by pointing out how angry he gets when another man catcalls his girlfriend or sister—or when a gay man catcalls him. Also, thinking back to my inability to flip off those catcallers in Saskatchewan all those years ago, I sometimes wonder if maybe gloves, not mittens, are properly feminist attire.

But men's misbehavior doesn't have to rise to the level of catcalling or other forms of harassment to make their belief in their entitlement of public space known. Take manspreading: in a crowded subway train or bus, there's one guy who's sitting spread-eagled taking up not only his own seat but most of those adjacent. Some men's rights activists have defended the practice, insisting that "it's physically painful for men to close their legs ... and it's also a biological necessity for us to do so."[11]* Other defenders of manspreading have recruited science, that manliest of disciplines, to argue that the practice is an "adaptive strategy that men employ due to innate morphological characteristics"—basically, the claim is that men's waist-to-shoulder ratio requires them to spread their knees out wide,

---

* How on earth MRAs think feminists can be unaware of the existence of balls, given that they think our entire modus operandi revolves around busting them, is beyond me. But consistency is the hobgoblin of little minds, I guess.

like "a cat's whiskers," to make sure there's enough room in the seat to accommodate the broadness of their shoulders.[12]* News flash: sitting spread-eagled is also more comfortable for female-bodied people, but most of us have been trained not to.†

Grant, then, the obnoxiousness of manspreading. The reason it's become a cultural flash point, I suspect—with blogs popping up dedicated to publicly shaming the perpetrators, and cities from New York to Madrid mounting PR campaigns condemning the practice on their public transit—is not just that it's a metaphor for toxic male entitlement. It's also that it can seem like there's nothing you can do to deal with a manspreader. Passive-aggressively refuse to give over the space in your seat and there's a risk the guy is going to interpret your leaning into him as a come-on. Directly confront him and there's a risk he'll escalate the situation into anger or even violence. Also, even if we're not afraid that the man will physically endanger us, women are still constrained by a lifetime of past socialization to be nice and not make a fuss.

But despair not! Allow me to let you in on a tactic that my sister, who just happens to be an infectious-diseases epidemiologist, stumbled upon. On her Toronto subway commute one day she was trapped in an inside seat by a guy who spread his legs wide enough to occupy half her seat in addition to his own. When she attempted to reclaim her space by refusing to shrink from his touch, he assumed that she was hitting on him and starting rubbing his arm against hers. No suitably polite Canadian rejoinder was coming to her, and, as any woman who's been in this situation knows, there's a possibility that a man like this will respond with anger or violence to direct confrontation. So my

---

* Why men's shoulders can't shoulder that tremendous responsibility all on their very own is unclear.

† I can't even tell you how many times I was told to "sit like a lady" as a child.

sister is sitting there, trying to make herself as small as possible and marinating in a brew of resentment and fear, and then she starts coughing.* And whaddaya know—the jerk recoils in disgust! Turns out he was capable of fitting into his own seat after all! And she realized that she'd found the antidote to manspreading. The brilliance of her coughing strategy, I think, lies in its plausible deniability. Anyone can summon up an unnerving cough while making it look unintentional.

How to Be an Ally (A Bonus Section for Men!)

OK, guys. You've made it this far in the book. Thanks for hanging in! You might be wondering what you can do to support more equal power for women on a personal level.

A basic first step is to spend more time listening than talking. Philosopher Bonnie Mann offers up some great advice here: you need to recognize that women are in a much better position than men to know what the problems with sexism are, because they're the ones who actually experience them.[13] So listen and don't interrupt. Be mindful that in many circumstances your voice will command more authority than a woman's simply because you're a man. Be circumspect about when and how to use this authority strategically, and when to pipe down so more women can be heard.

Mann also counsels men to be aware of the ways you're implicated in the patriarchal world order. Understand that while you might never have harassed a woman, the men who have harassed or even raped a woman are acting within the same male-privileged society you do. It might be tempting to demonize the men who harass or rape women, but it's important to

---

* It's the middle of a Canadian winter. Everyone has a cold.

realize that these are just men who take seriously the perks and entitlements granted them by a world from which you also benefit. When you challenge the actions of these men, Mann writes, you need to see them as *peers*.

> Understanding that portraying certain men (often racially coded) as monsters amounts to engaging in a kind of public relations campaign for masculinism as a whole, allies avoid such portrayals.... They will not approach the harasser as an individual monster, then, but as a co-beneficiary of a system that is not of their own, individual, making—knowing that they, too, have to be vigilant against enacting its privileges.... Allies are not princes in shining armor, they are culture critics.[14]

GET BETTER AT FLIRTING

"Don't sexually harass or assault women" is the obvious advice here, but it's not enough. Even though most straight men (cis or trans) don't sexually harass or assault women, they still need to recognize that there's a very good chance that the women they approach have experienced some form of sexual harassment or violence at some point in their lives.

Armed with this knowledge, how should you engage with a woman you like? How do you make your interest known without being creepy? What about all the ambiguity and nuance and innuendo and subtlety that can characterize flirting? Do we have an obligation to forgo most of this in the name of making sure that we're not participating in or perpetuating the problematic elements of our sexual culture? If everyone's internalized their respective gender roles in a world that's eroticized masculine dominance and feminine submission, is feminist-friendly heterosexual flirtation possible?

Happily, Mann insists that it is. The key, she says, is to aim for a situation where the power between the two parties is roughly equal, so that both are equally vulnerable. Mann's exemplar of feminist-friendly flirtation comes from the 1991 film *Thelma and Louise*. In it, Thelma (Geena Davis) picks up JD, a hitchhiker (Brad Pitt, in a breakout role).* No one could accuse them of offering up wildly novel or unconventional depictions of masculinity or femininity. But throughout their flirtation (and eventual steamy sex scene), JD is respectful, playful, patient, and "clearly open to the possibility that [Thelma's] hesitation is the final word on the encounter."[15] This flirtation "is invitation and appeal, not demand. It requires vigilance against acquisitiveness and entitlement."[16] If JD can do it, gentlemen, you can too.

So if you're looking for an instruction manual for how to interact with a woman you're interested in sexually, here are a few thoughts: Slow down. Don't act or feel like you're entitled to set the terms of the encounter. Try to find out what a woman wants. Ask questions. Ask permission. Be OK with the possibility that you might be rejected. Appreciate that our culture makes a woman significantly more vulnerable than you, so give her the power in this situation.

FORGET ABOUT CHIVALRY

I know, I know. "But my mama taught me to be chivalrous! She'd be horrified if I stopped! She'd never forgive me if I dropped

---

* You can google the sex scenes if you're impatient, but if you haven't seen this movie (ever, or in years) I cannot recommend highly enough that you watch the whole thing. It's not perfect—there are still plenty of tired tropes of the sexy bad boy, and the ending doesn't exactly inspire hope about whether it's possible for women to flourish after they've shed patriarchal constraints—but the movie's depiction of Thelma moving from victim of sexual assault to a woman in control of her sexual agency and desires serves as a prescient model for today's MeToo moment.

this stuff just because some bossy feminist told me to!" Wrong. What your mama was trying to teach you was how to be respectful toward women. In contrast, chivalrous gestures serve little practical purpose. Their purpose is primarily symbolic. They send the message that women are incapable and helpless and that men are the ones with power.

On their own, individual chivalrous actions—things like holding a door open for a woman, or picking up the check on a date, or walking between her and the street so her purse isn't snatched and she isn't splashed with mud from cars—are purported to be gestures of helpfulness, politeness, or respect. But women don't usually need men to hold doors open for us; we're perfectly capable of opening doors for ourselves. Women wouldn't need men to pay for dinner if the wage gap didn't put them two steps ahead of us all the time. Women wouldn't need protection from purse snatchers and traffic filth if our fashion were as practical and affordable as men's.

Let me be clear: I'm not suggesting that men should stop holding doors open for women. I'm just insisting that they make sure they're doing it for the right reasons. I'm Canadian! We think holding a door open for someone if you've gotten there first is required by basic human decency. I'm pretty sure it's been written into our Charter of Rights and Freedoms. But if you're holding a door open for reasons of Canadian politeness then you're willing to have it held open for you as well, and you're willing to open it for everyone regardless of gender expression. When a feminist gets agitated about a door being held open for her, it's not the gesture itself but the suspected motivation of exerting male dominance she's taking issue with. Rather than getting indignant, a guy just needs to allow her to extend the same courtesy.

Women don't need the protections of chivalry. What we *do* need is men who are willing to fight patriarchy; men who are willing to consider giving up the privileges they've received strictly because of their gender; men who don't think that relinquishing this unearned privilege is an injustice.

How to Be Real

But let's be honest, ladies: many of us don't really want men to entirely quit with the chivalry, do we? I like it when my boyfriend pays for dinner and spoils me with presents. I like it when he schleps my too-heavy suitcase for me, even though we both know I'm capable of carrying it myself. And I like these things not just because they're romantic and sweet—I like them *because* they're gendered. We have both internalized these romantic scripts and find pleasure in playing our gendered roles.

Along these same lines, I usually enjoy performing my femme identity. Makeup can be fun. Cute shoes are delightful. I won't pretend not to feel a rush of glee when I catch a glimpse of myself in a mirror and I'm feeling pretty that day. I've gone through phases where my feminist indignation about the amount of time and money I was expected to sink into these pursuits made me stop indulging in these narcissistic delights. Without fail, my self-esteem would tank. It didn't matter if every feminist bone in my body knew how much unnecessary energy I was wasting on this frippery: I hated myself without it. Eventually I'd decide it wasn't worth it to not feel like myself and I'd return to the frivolities. I've been pretty good about not falling prey to the bad-faith pretense that I want to look and dress like this "for myself"—because, c'mon, if we're honest with ourselves, dressing for ourselves looks like yoga pants and fuzzy sweaters, not stilettos and push-up bras. But that I let myself do this doesn't mean I don't often wish I didn't feel like I have to.

What I've decided on, over more than four decades as a feminist femme, is a strategy perhaps best described as candid ambivalence. I try to admit that the person I want to be, the person *I am*, is a person whose fundamental desires and sense of self have been messed up by the sexist norms and expectations of a patriarchal world order that I'm committed to dismantling—that I am this way because I've taken on board a stunted and limiting story about what women are good for. And I understand that my conventional performances of cis white femininity *harm other women*—women who, for reasons of racism, or ableism, or classism, or transphobia, pay the price because they cannot or will not live up to the standards I affirm by my behavior and thus reinforce in the culture at large.

My strategy of ambivalence here has been inspired by one gestured at by Sandra Bartky. Analyzing the hypothetical case of a woman whose masochistic sexual fantasies are fundamentally at odds with her feminist political commitments, Bartky argues that such a woman is "entitled to her shame."[17] It's not that this woman *ought* to feel shame, exactly—certainly not in the finger-wagging, "You should be ashamed of yourself!" sense of the word. But neither is it that she ought not to feel shame: "her desires are not worthy of her, after all, nor is it clear that she is a mere helpless victim of patriarchal conditioning, unable to take any responsibility at all for her wishes and fantasies."[18] It makes sense for this woman to feel shame, Bartky thinks, because "shame is a wholly understandable response to behavior that is seriously at variance with principles."[19]

Anytime people put on clothes they are performing a (usually) gendered identity. But try to be aware of how your appearance works toward or against patriarchal culture. Only you can decide whether it's in conflict with your political principles and what to do if it is. Do what you can to make your performances of gender your own. "If I didn't define myself for myself," wrote Audre Lorde, "I would be crunched into other people's fantasies for me and eaten alive."[20] Remember, as Uma Narayan puts it, that we're all bargaining with patriarchy.

But at the end of the day, don't pretend that everything's fine when it's not. Don't pretend that you're fine when you're not. When you do that you minimize the harms of this misogynistic world order. Recognize that any insistence that your performance of femininity is done for its own sake, that it's being turned in without any interest in whether it's attractive to men (or anyone else), is likely not taking seriously the deep connections between femininity and objectification. Admit that you've been messed up, that you are damaged goods, that some of your deepest, most identity-conferring priorities and commitments have been warped by precisely those forces of sexism you're committed to destroying. But you might decide this isn't the hill worth dying on. Maybe all the navel-gazing on a therapist's couch it would take to excise this particular incarnation of patriarchy's grip on your soul isn't the best use of your feminist energies—maybe you'd be better off just slapping on some lipstick and getting to the rape-crisis hotline you volunteer at on time.

Better to pick your best battles and make the changes you can.

WHY NOT HUMANISM?

Something you often hear from the "I'm not a feminist, but" types is that instead of "feminists" we should call ourselves "humanists." "Feminism," in their view, is a label that's too far gone, too weighted down with the intimation that the collective goal here is the establishment of a matriarchy where women smear menstrual blood all over their bodies and howl at the moon to honor the Wiccan Mother Goddess and only bother keeping men around to work as sex slaves and maybe do some manual labor. Even if the entirety of human history has been characterized by men having the upper hand, two wrongs don't make a right, they scold.

"Humanism," on the other hand, implies equality. And who doesn't like equality?

To which I say: bullshit. The reason we will need "feminism" instead of "humanism" for the foreseeable future is that the latter risks ignoring thousands of years of history, risks pretending that we've already achieved gender equality when we obviously have not. If and when feminism is actually successful in achieving gender equality it won't need to exist anymore. (Yep. You heard me right: feminism's goal is to eradicate the need for its own existence.) Maybe another way to put it is that feminism's goal is humanism. But to insist on humanism now is to pretend that we live in a radically different world than we actually do.

Objectification, misogyny, the male gaze, gender essentialism, rape culture, and sexist oppression have a long and storied history. The process of dismantling them will be equally epic and enduring. The patriarchy will not be overthrown in my lifetime, or in my daughter's, or her daughter's. The catcalls and pussy-grabbing and mansplaining and sexual violence will continue. But we can, and we will, make progress, and my hope is that, having read *Think Like a Feminist*, you'll have a better handle on the reality of the situation. My hope is that you'll be able to grasp and make sense of the double-binds you experience, the false expectations you have to confront, the wires of the birdcage you're surrounded by. My hope is that you'll never again have to feel like you're entirely alone in trying to shake free.

AFTERWORD TO THE PAPERBACK EDITION

I thought I had things figured out before 2020. I wrote *Think Like a Feminist* cognizant of the feminist movement's historical failures, quick to admit its misguided tendency to center the experiences of white, straight, cis, able-bodied, wealthy, and middle-class women, determined to avoid repeating these past mistakes. I knew the book needed to be, at its core, a work of intersectional feminism—a book that understood that people with multiple marginalized social identities experience oppression that is both qualitatively and quantitatively different from those with fewer, and that these same marginalized people are often uniquely situated to both diagnose the problems in our social world and to create novel solutions to them. I went to the mat against TERFs, insisting that their attempts to exclude trans women from the feminist movement were no different from Betty Friedan and other mainstream second-wave feminists' exclusions of lesbians and women of color, insisting that trans women have something important to teach us about performing femininity in a culture that hates women. I leaned heavily on the theoretical insights of black feminists like Audre Lorde and bell hooks, and Latinx feminists like Maria Lugones. I thought I'd done my best to avoid feminism's old pitfalls, that I'd shown that it's possible to keep feminism moving forward. But it turns out that living through a once-in-a-generation civil rights uprising and a once-in-a-century pandemic in the same year has a funny way of driving these lessons home in a new way.

2020 was the year that women like me figured out that the "second shift" had been a gentle warm-up to what capitalism was willing to demand from us in offloading the work of raising the next generation of cogs for its machine. I spent much of the spring holed up in my apartment with my cat and then seven-year-old daughter, cajoling the latter into submitting to online schooling, permitting a heretofore unimaginable amount of screen time, concocting ghost hunts, and running laps up and down the hallways together when she got too stir-crazy. I counted myself lucky to have a stable job and health insurance, even while I took on the thankless task of shifting my university teaching online while I worked through unpaid furlough days. Already well-versed in navigating the gendered asymmetries of domestic labor, once the pandemic's stay-at-home orders set in, many straight working women found themselves forced back into domestic roles they could no longer outsource, backsliding on the slight amounts of progress their generation might have made in the domestic sphere. And 2020 was the year that even the wealthiest straight men, trapped in their homes with their families, were for the briefest of moments forced to figure out how much work it takes to raise a child, how difficult it is to do this work well, and how much they had been exploiting the mothers, housecleaners, childcare workers, and teachers previously tasked with most of this labor.

Unsurprisingly, wealthier families were able to find their way out of the worst of it relatively quickly. Many public schools in wealthier areas (not to mention private schools) had kids back in the classroom in person by the fall, held up as shining examples of what was possible when teachers and administrators were willing to "get creative" in reconfiguring classroom spaces to permit social distancing. Left unspoken was the brutal reality that overcrowded and underfunded schools in poorer districts had no hope of enacting these creative strategies; their students would go on to spend the entire school year struggling online. 2020 could have been the year we figured out how to finally start addressing the educational disparities attached to income inequality in this country, when we could have explored radical new visions for childcare and eldercare that revolutionized our collective approach to the sick and vulnerable among us. Instead, we saw an awful lot of progressive energy spent bemoaning how much more difficult it had become for white businesswomen striving to make their way up the corporate ladder.

2020 was the year that queers like me figured out the need for Pride to put BIPOC first. I spent the second Saturday in June walking down the middle of Hollywood Boulevard in Los Angeles. Despite the Pride parade, like so much else that year, being officially cancelled, there were thousands of us who marched anyhow, passing out masks and hand sanitizer, linking arms down the street and shouting, "Black Trans Lives Matter" to the refrains of N.W.A.'s "FTP" and Nipsey Hussle's "FDT." Signs in the crowd read "Sex is good, but have you ever fucked the system?" and "Racism is small dick energy." 2020 was the year that queers were reminded that our collective priorities need to go beyond securing marriage equality for those who want a slightly less heteronormative version of the minivan and white picket fence, that the members of our community who are most at risk face not just homophobia but also the intersecting oppressions of racism, ableism, classism, and transphobia.

2020 was the year that white people like me figured out that it was no longer possible to stay home in the face of brutal racial oppression—when the police brutality, the racial profiling, the mass incarceration faced by black and brown people finally took center stage in our collective consciousness. An estimated fifteen to twenty-six million people protested that summer. My daughter declared the colorful chants at the adult protests to be superior to the sanitized kids' versions, then while listening to her beloved *Hamilton* soundtrack one afternoon asked, "Mama, why do they call him a 'bastard'? He wasn't a cop." When people's inboxes and social media feeds filled up with concern-trolling friends and family tut-tutting, "Who protests during a pandemic?" they doubled down on the masks and hand sanitizer and took solace in the words of Audre Lorde: "Sometimes we are blessed with being able to choose the time, and the arena, and the manner of our revolution, but more usually we must do battle where we are standing." Throughout 2020, black and brown people caught and died of COVID in disproportionate numbers, faced medical mistreatment in disproportionate numbers, faced unemployment and poverty in disproportionate numbers, faced eviction in disproportionate numbers. They risked their lives as low-paid frontline essential workers in disproportionate numbers while their kids languished in virtual classrooms in disproportionate numbers. But 2020 was also the year that racialized injustices like these were no longer swept under the rug. It remains to be seen whether the outcry over the deaths of George Floyd and Breonna Taylor and so many others will have the kind of lasting changes on our culture's treatment of black and brown people that many were fighting for, but at least for a moment the world started paying attention.

Kimberlé Crenshaw is best known for her metaphor that makes sense of the experience of living with multiple oppressed identities as akin to the perils of navigating a snarled traffic intersection. But I think it's her less familiar basement metaphor that deserves renewed attention after the collective experiences of 2020. This metaphor reminds us that the power dynamics of oppression don't stop functioning within liberation movements. It reminds us that those who are more disadvantaged by their marginalized social identities are often crushed under the feet of those whose social identities face less oppression. It reminds us that too often these movements have only really cared about those who "but for" one or two identities wouldn't need help at all. The basement metaphor reminds us that **the whole point of social justice is to make the world better for those who are worse off than we are**.

Remembering this, I am convinced, is how to think like a feminist.

ACKNOWLEDGMENTS

I'd like to thank a number of professional colleagues for conversations, feedback, and advice on this project or those that led up to it, including Ásta, Louise Antony, Amy Baehr, Ken Barton, Elvira Basevich, Nancy Bauer, Maren Behrensen, Samantha Brennan, Annie Cahill, Ann Cudd, Robin Dembroff, Esa Díaz-León, Robin Dillon, Andre Dubus III, Elizabeth Edenberg, Carla Fehr, Ann Garry, Lori Gruen, Sally Haslanger, Diana Heney, Grayson Hunt, Alison Jaggar, Aaron James, Katharine Jenkins, Alison Kerr, Serene Khader, Quill Kukla, Alice MacLachlan, Rachel MacKinnon, Kate Manne, Clancy Martin, Emily McGill, José Mendoza, Sarah Clark Miller, Charles Mills, Cathy Muller, Kate Norlock, Nico Orlandi, Julinna Oxley, Serena Parekh, Sandra Raponi, Joel Reynolds, Ruth Sample, Naomi Scheman, Alexis Shotwell, Daniel Silvermint, David Smith, Subrena Smith, Susanne Sreedhar, Jason Stanley, Anita Superson, Sigrún Svavarsdóttir, Lynne Tirrell, Helga Varden, Lori Watson, Justin Weinberg, Amelia Wirts, and Charlotte Witt.

For indispensable guidance, advice, and killer editing chops, I thank Amy Cherry, my editor at Norton, and her assistant,

Zarina Patwa; Markus Hoffman, my agent; and Peter Catapano at the *Times*.

Thanks also to audiences at Coastal Carolina University, Fordham University, University of Kentucky, and Trinity College, and to my many students over the years, particularly those in UML's spring 2019 section of Feminist Theory.

And finally, eternal gratitude to my friends, family, and favorites for love and support, for snuggles and kicks in the ass: Sheila Busch, Ana Paula Carneiro (my baby's second mama), Margaret Darling, Jill Goldman (my teacher), Maria Halovanic, Brian Hay, Jame Hay, Karen HayDraude, Jeremy HayDraude, Becky Kaag, John Kaag, Becca Kaag-Hay (my little bear), Jaime Kelly, Junior Lombardi, M (for treats), Eliza Malta, Alice MacLachlan (No Committee member extraordinaire), José Mendoza, N (*il mio amore*), P (for spanks), Shippen Page, Kelli Parker, Maxine Pirie, Ken Pope, Tess Pope, Madhava Setty, Susanne Sreedhar (my zero-bullshit ride-or-die), Anne St. Goar, Helga Varden, Sarah Vitelli, Bobbi Vogel, Lori Watson, and Amelia Wirts.

NOTES

PREFACE

1. Caitlyn Flanagan, "The Humiliation of Aziz Ansari," *The Atlantic,* January 2018, accessed November 11, 2019, https://www.theatlantic.com/entertainment/archive/2018/01/the-humiliation-of-aziz-ansari/550541/.
2. Katie Roiphe, "The New Whisper Network," *Harpers*, March 2018, accessed November 11, 2019, https://harpers.org/archive/2018/03/the-other-whisper-network-2/?single=1.

CHAPTER 1: THE F-WORD

1. John Stuart Mill, "The Subjection of Women," in John Stuart Mill and Harriet Taylor Mill, *Essays on Sex Equality*, ed. Alice Rossi (Chicago: University of Chicago Press, 1970 [1869]), 130.
2. Shulamith Firestone, *The Dialectic of Sex* (New York: William Morrow & Company, 1970).
3. David Buss, *The Evolution of Desire: Strategies of Human Mating*, 4th ed. (New York: Basic Books, 2016 [1995]), 211.
4. Leslie Goldstein, "Early Feminist Themes in French Utopian Socialism: The St.-Simonians and Fourier," *Journal of the History of Ideas* 43, no. 1 (1982): 91–108.
5. Karl Marx and Frederick Engels, *The Communist Manifesto* (Chicago: Charles H. Kerr & Co, 1906 [1848]), 59.

6. Charles Fourier, *The Theory of the Four Movements*, eds. and trans. Gareth Stedman Jones and Ian Patterson (Cambridge: Cambridge University Press, 1996 [1808]), 132. Italics in original.

7. Charles Fourier, *Oeuvres Complètes de Charles Fourier*, 12 vols. (Paris: Anthropos, 1966–1968): vol. 1, 130–31, 149–50; vol. 6, 191.

8. Karen Offen, *European Feminisms, 1700–1950: A Political History* (Stanford: Stanford University Press, 1999).

9. Betty Friedan, *The Feminine Mystique* (New York: W. W. Norton & Co., 2013 [1963]), 57.

10. Rebecca Walker, "Becoming the Third Wave," *Ms.*, January/February 1992, 39–41.

11. See, e.g., Chandra Talpade Mohanty, "Under Western Eyes: Feminist Scholarship and Colonial Discourses," *boundary 2* 12, no. 3 (1984): 333–58; Uma Narayan, "Minds of Their Own: Choices, Autonomy, Cultural Practices and Other Women," in *A Mind of One's Own: Feminist Essays on Reason and Objectivity*, 2nd ed., eds. Louise Antony and Charlotte Witt (Boulder, CO: Westview Press, 2002); and Alison Jaggar, "'Saving Amina': Global Justice for Women and Intercultural Dialogue," *Ethics and International Affairs* 19, no. 3 (2005): 55–75.

12. Narayan, "Minds of Their Own," 222.

13. Gayatri Spivak, "Can the Subaltern Speak?: Speculations on Widow Sacrifice," *Wedge* 7/8 (1985): 120–30.

14. Valerie Solanas, *SCUM Manifesto* (New York: Verso, 2004 [1967]), 35.

15. Pat Robertson, fundraising letter for Christian Coalition, as quoted in Associated Press, "Robertson Letter Attacks Feminists," *The New York Times*, August 26, 1992, accessed November 11, 2019, https://www.nytimes.com/1992/08/26/us/robertson-letter-attacks-feminists.html.

16. Jordan Peterson, interview by Helen Lewis, *British GQ*, January 15, 2019, accessed November 11, 2019, https://www.gq-magazine.co.uk/article/jordan-peterson-interview-2018.

17. Andrea Dworkin, *Our Blood: Prophecies and Discourses on Sexual Politics* (New York: Harper & Row, 1976), 78.

18. Simone de Beauvoir, *The Second Sex*, ed. and trans. H. M. Parshley (New York: Vintage, 1989 [1949]), xvii.

19. Sandra Bartky, "Foucault, Femininity, and the Modernization of Patriarchal Power," *Femininity and Domination: Studies in the Phenomenology of Oppression* (New York: Routledge, 1990), 78.

20. Camille Paglia, *Sex, Art, and American Culture: Essays* (New York: Knopf Doubleday, 2011), 264.

21. bell hooks, *Killing Rage: Ending Racism* (New York: Henry Holt, 1996 [1995]), 8–11.

22. Audre Lorde, "The Uses of Anger: Women Responding to Racism," in *Sister Outsider*, 2nd ed. (New York: Ten Speed Press, 2007 [1984]), 125.

23. Sarah Ahmed, *Living a Feminist Life* (Durham, NC: Duke University Press, 2017), 255.

24. Lorde, "Uses of Anger," 131.

25. Rebecca Traister, *Good and Mad: The Revolutionary Power of Women's Anger* (New York: Simon & Schuster, 2018), xx.

26. Traister, *Good and Mad*, xx–xxii.

27. A Woman's Nation, *The Shriver Report Snapshot: An Insight into the 21st Century Man*, April 23, 2015, accessed November 11, 2019, http://www.shrivermedia.com/wp-content/uploads/2016/05/FINAL-Shriver-Report-Snapshot-Press-Release.pdf.

28. Traister, *Good and Mad*, 10.

29. Ariel Levy, *Female Chauvinist Pigs: Women and the Rise of Raunch Culture* (New York: Free Press, 2006).

30. Andrea Dworkin, "Dworkin on Dworkin," in *Radically Speaking: Feminism Reclaimed,* eds. Renate Klein and Diane Bell (North Melbourne: Spinifex Press, 1996), 272.

31. Paglia, *Sex, Art and American Culture,* 50.

32. Linda Hirshman, *Get to Work: A Manifesto for Women of the World* (New York: Penguin, 2006).

33. Jessa Crispin, *Why I Am Not a Feminist* (Brooklyn, NY: Melville House, 2017), xiii.

34. Crispin, *Why I Am Not a Feminist*, 147.

35. "Women Now Empowered by Everything a Woman Does," *The Onion,* accessed November 11, 2019, https://www.theonion.com/women-now-empowered-by-everything-a-woman-does-1819566746.

CHAPTER 2: OPPRESSION

1. Marilyn Frye, *The Politics of Reality* (Berkeley: Crossing Press, 1983), 4–5.

2. Ariane Hegewisch and Heidi Hartmann, "The Gender Wage Gap: 2018 Earnings Differences by Race and Ethnicity," Institute for Women's Pol-

icy Research, March 7, 2019, accessed November 11, 2019, https://iwpr
.org/publications/gender-wage-gap-2018/.

3. Susan Brownmiller, *Against Our Will: Men, Women and Rape* (New York:
   Simon and Schuster, 1975).

4. Iris Marion Young, "Five Faces of Oppression," in *Justice and the Politics
   of Difference* (Princeton: Princeton University Press, 2011 [1990]), 41.

5. Sally Haslanger, "Oppressions: Racial and Other," in *Resisting Reality:
   Social Construction and Social Critique* (Oxford: Oxford University
   Press, 2012), 311–40.

6. David Foster Wallace, *This Is Water: Some Thoughts, Delivered on a Significant Occasion, About Living a Compassionate Life* (New York: Little,
   Brown & Co., 2009), 117.

7. Peggy McIntosh, "White Privilege: Unpacking the Invisible Knapsack,"
   Peace and Freedom, July/August 1989, 10–12.

8. McIntosh, "Unpacking the Invisible Knapsack," 10.

9. Barack Obama, "Remarks by the President on Trayvon Martin,"
   press release, July 19, 2013, accessed November 11, 2019, https://
   obamawhitehouse.archives.gov/the-press-office/2013/07/19/remarks
   -president-trayvon-martin.

10. Michel Foucault, *Discipline and Punish: The Birth of the Prison* (New
    York: Pantheon, 1977), 155.

11. Sandra Bartky, "Foucault, Femininity, and the Modernization of Patriar-
    chal Power," in *Femininity and Domination: Studies in the Phenomenol-
    ogy of Oppression* (New York: Routledge, 1990), 80.

12. Andrea Dworkin, *Woman Hating* (Boston: E. P. Dutton, 1974), 113–14.

13. Mary Wollstonecraft, *A Vindication of the Rights of Woman* (New York:
    Oxford University Press, 1993 [1792]), 111–12.

14. Iris Marion Young, "Throwing Like a Girl: A Phenomenology of Femi-
    nine Body Comportment Motility and Spatiality," *Human Studies* (1980),
    137–56.

15. Young, "Throwing Like a Girl," 148.

16. Young, "Throwing Like a Girl," 144.

17. W. E. B. Du Bois, *The Souls of Black Folk* (Chicago: A. C. McClurg & Co.,
    1907 [1903]), 3.

18. Bartky, "Modernization of Patriarchal Power," 72.

19. Laura Mulvey, "Visual Pleasure and Narrative Cinema," *Screen* 16, no. 3
    (1975): 6–18.

20. Catharine MacKinnon, *Toward a Feminist Theory of the State* (Cambridge: Harvard University Press, 1989), 149.

21. John Elster, *Sour Grapes: Studies in the Subversion of Rationality* (Cambridge: Cambridge University Press, 1985).

22. Susan Bordo, "Feminism, Foucault and the Politics of the Body," *Up Against Foucault: Explorations of Some Tensions Between Foucault and Feminism*, ed. Caroline Ramazanoglu (New York: Routledge, 1993), 189–90.

23. Bordo, "Feminism, Foucault and the Politics of the Body," 192.

24. Bertrand Russell, *How to Be Free and Happy* (New York: The Rand School of Social Science, 1924).

25. Ann Cudd, *Analyzing Oppression* (New York: Oxford University Press, 2006), 22. Also see Ann Cudd, "Strikes, Housework, and the Moral Obligation to Resist," *Journal of Social Philosophy* 29 (1998): 20–36; and Ann Cudd, "Oppression by Choice," *Journal of Social Philosophy* 25 (1994): 22–44.

26. Susan Brownmiller, *Against Our Will: Men, Women and Rape* (New York: Simon & Schuster, 1975).

27. Sandra Bartky, "Feminine Masochism and the Politics of Personal Transformation," *Femininity and Domination: Studies in the Phenomenology of Oppression* (New York: Routledge, 1990), 51.

28. Uma Narayan, "Minds of Their Own: Choices, Autonomy, Cultural Practices and Other Women," in *A Mind of One's Own: Feminist Essays on Reason and Objectivity*, 2nd ed., eds. Louise Antony and Charlotte Witt (Boulder, CO: Westview Press, 2002), 202.

29. Kimberlé Crenshaw, "Demarginalizing the Intersection of Race and Sex: A Black Feminist Critique of Antidiscrimination Doctrine, Feminist Theory, and Antiracist Politics," *University of Chicago Legal Forum* 1 (1989): 149.

30. Elizabeth Spelman, *Inessential Woman: Problems of Exclusion in Feminist Thought* (Boston: Beacon Press, 1988).

31. Spelman, *Inessential Woman*, 136.

32. María Lugones, *Pilgrimages/Peregrinajes: Theorizing Coalition Against Multiple Oppressions* (Lanham, MD: Rowman & Littlefield, 2003).

33. Lugones, *Pilgrimages/Peregrinajes*, 123.

34. Lugones, *Pilgrimages/Peregrinajes*, 145.

35. Crenshaw, "A Black Feminist Critique," 151–52.

36. Audre Lorde, "The Uses of Anger: Women Responding to Racism," in *Sister Outsider*, 2nd ed. (New York: Ten Speed Press, 2007 [1984]), 132.

37. bell hooks, *Feminist Theory: From Margin to Center* (Brooklyn: South End Press, 1984), 3.

38. Moya Zakia Bailey, *Race, Region, and Gender in Early Emory School of Medicine Yearbooks* (Dissertation Thesis, 2013), 26.

39. Kesiena Boom, "4 Tired Tropes That Perfectly Explain What Misogynoir Is—And How You Can Stop It," *Everyday Feminism*, August 3, 2016, accessed November 11, 2019, https://everydayfeminism.com/2015/08/4 -tired-tropes-misogynoir/.

40. MiQuel Davies, "Racism in Health Care—For Black Women Who Become Pregnant, It's a Matter of Life and Death," National Women's Law Center, April 13, 2018, accessed November 11, 2019, https://nwlc.org/blog/ racism-in-health-care-for-black-women-who-become-pregnant-its-a -matter-of-life-and-death/.

41. Kimberlé Crenshaw, "Beyond Racism and Misogyny: Black Feminism and 2 Live Crew," *Boston Review*, December 1991, 9.

42. Frances Beale, "Double Jeopardy: To Be Black and Female," *The Black Woman: An Anthology*, ed. Toni Cade (New York: New American Library, 1970), 90–100.

43. Patricia Hill Collins, *Black Feminist Thought: Knowledge, Consciousness and the Politics of Empowerment* (New York: Routledge, 1990).

44. Alice Walker, *In Search of Our Mothers' Gardens: Womanist Prose* (London: Phoenix, 2005 [1983]), xii.

45. Audre Lorde, "The Master's Tools Will Never Dismantle the Master's House," in *Sister Outsider*, 2nd ed. (New York: Ten Speed Press, 2007 [1984]), 112. Emphasis removed.

CHAPTER 3: THE SOCIAL CONSTRUCTION OF GENDER

1. Aristotle, *Historia Animālium*, ed. and trans. A. L. Peck (Cambridge: Harvard University Press, 1970), 608b 1–14.

2. Simone de Beauvoir, *The Second Sex*, ed. and trans. H. M. Parshley (New York: Vintage, 1989 [1949]), xxi.

3. Linda Nicholson, "Interpreting Gender," *Signs* 20, no. 1 (1994): 79–105; and Linda Nicholson, "Gender," in *A Companion to Feminist Philosophy*,

eds. Alison Jaggar and Iris Marion Young (Malden, MA: Blackwell Publishers, 1998), 289–98.

4. R. J. Stoller, *Sex and Gender: On the Development of Masculinity and Femininity* (New York: Science House, 1968).

5. Lise Eliot, *Pink Brain, Blue Brain: How Small Differences Grow into Troublesome Gaps—And What We Can Do About It* (New York: Houghton Mifflin Harcourt, 2009), 10.

6. Cordelia Fine, *Delusions of Gender: How Our Minds, Society, and Neurosexism Create Difference* (New York: W. W. Norton & Co., 2010); and Cordelia Fine, *Testosterone Rex: Myths of Sex, Science, and Society* (New York: W. W. Norton & Co., 2017).

7. Marilyn Frye, *The Politics of Reality* (Berkeley: Crossing Press, 1983), 37.

8. T. D. Conley, A. C. Moors, J. L. Matsick, A. Ziegler, and B. A. Valentine, "Women, Men, and the Bedroom: Methodological and Conceptual Insights That Narrow, Reframe, and Eliminate Gender Differences in Sexuality," *Current Directions in Psychological Science* 20, no. 5 (2011), 296–300.

9. de Beauvoir, *The Second Sex*, 267. Emphasis added.

10. Gayle Rubin, "The Traffic in Women: Notes on the 'Political Economy' of Sex" in *Toward an Anthropology of Women*, ed. Rayna R. Reiter (New York: Monthly Review Press, 1975), 159.

11. Nicholson, "Interpreting Gender," 81.

12. Nancy Chodorow, *The Reproduction of Mothering: Psychoanalysis and the Sociology of Gender* (Berkeley: University of California Press, 1978).

13. See, e.g., Peggy Orenstein, *Cinderella Ate My Daughter: Dispatches from the Front Lines of the New Girlie-Girl Culture* (New York: Harper Collins, 2011); Eliot, *Pink Brain, Blue Brain*; and Fine, *Delusions of Gender* and *Testosterone Rex*.

14. Judith Butler, "Performative Acts and Gender Constitution: An Essay in Phenomenology and Feminist Theory," *Theatre Journal* 40, no. 4 (1988): 519–31; and Judith Butler, *Gender Trouble: Feminism and the Subversion of Identity* (New York: Routledge, 1990).

15. Frye, *Politics of Reality*, 29.

16. Fine, *Delusions of Gender* and *Testosterone Rex*.

17. Claire Renzetti and Daniel Curran, "Gender Socialization," in *Feminist Philosophies: Problems, Theories, and Applications*, eds. Janet

Kourany, James Sterba, and Rosemarie Tong (London: Prentice Hall, 1992), 31–48.

18. Eliot, *Pink Brain, Blue Brain*; and Fine, *Delusions of Gender* and *Testosterone Rex*.

19. Carol Gilligan, *In a Different Voice: Psychological Theory and Women's Development* (Cambridge: Harvard University Press, 1982); Nel Noddings, *Caring: A Feminine Approach to Ethics and Moral Education* (Berkeley: University of California Press, 1984).

20. Susan Griffin, *Made from This Earth: An Anthology of Writings* (New York: Harper & Row, 1982); Mary Daly, *Gyn/ecology: The Metaethics of Radical Feminism*, 2nd ed. (Boston: Beacon Press, 1990 [1978]); Starhawk, *The Spiral Dance: A Rebirth of the Ancient Religion of the Great Goddess* (San Francisco: Harper & Row, 1979).

21. Sally Haslanger, "(What) Are Race and Gender? (What) Do We Want Them To Be?," in *Resisting Reality: Social Construction and Social Critique* (Oxford: Oxford University Press, 2012), 221–47.

22. Frye, *Politics of Reality*, 22ff.

23. John Stuart Mill, "The Subjection of Women," in John Stuart Mill and Harriet Taylor Mill, *Essays on Sex Equality*, ed. Alice Rossi (Chicago: University of Chicago Press, 1970 [1869]), 451.

24. Mill, "Subjection of Women," 451.

25. Kate Millett, *Sexual Politics* (New York: Columbia University Press, 1969), 26.

26. Haslanger, "Race and Gender," 230.

27. Catharine MacKinnon, *Toward a Feminist Theory of the State* (Cambridge: Harvard University Press, 1989), 113.

CHAPTER 4: THE SOCIAL CONSTRUCTION OF SEX

1. Simone de Beauvoir, *The Second Sex*, ed. and trans. H. M. Parshley (New York: Vintage, 1989 [1949]), 267.

2. Marilyn Frye, *The Politics of Reality* (Berkeley: Crossing Press, 1983), 46.

3. John Stuart Mill, "The Subjection of Women," in John Stuart Mill and Harriet Taylor Mill, *Essays on Sex Equality*, ed. Alice Rossi (Chicago: University of Chicago Press, 1970 [1869]), 49.

4. Mill, "Subjection of Women," 49–50.

5. Louise M. Antony, "Natures and Norms," *Ethics* 111, no. 1 (2000): 8–36.

6. Elizabeth Spelman, *Inessential Woman: Problems of Exclusion in Feminist Thought* (Boston: Beacon Press, 1988), 159.

7. Spelman, *Inessential Woman*, 13.

8. Chandra Mohanty, "'Under Western Eyes' Revisited: Feminist Solidarity Through Anticapitalist Struggles," *Signs* 28, no. 2 (2003), 518.

9. Judith Butler, *Gender Trouble: Feminism and the Subversion of Identity* (New York: Routledge, 1990), 160.

10. See, e.g., Theodore Bach, 2012, "Gender Is a Natural Kind with a Historical Essence," *Ethics* 122 (2012): 231–72; Natalie Stoljar, "Essence, Identity and the Concept of Woman," *Philosophical Topics* 23, no. 2 (1995): 261–94.

11. Martha Nussbaum, "The Professor of Parody: The Hip Defeatism of Judith Butler," *The New Republic*, February 22, 1999, 45–48. Also see Susan Bordo, "Material Girl: The Effacements of Postmodern Culture," *Michigan Quarterly Review*, 29, no.4 (1990): 653–78, and Susan Bordo, "Postmodern Subjects, Postmodern Bodies: A Review Essay," *Feminist Studies* 18, no. 1 (1991): 159–76.

12. See, e.g., Nancy Fraser, *Fortunes of Feminism: From Women's Liberation to Identity Politics to Anti-Capitalism* (New York: Verso, 2013), and Nussbaum, "The Professor of Parody."

13. Ludwig Wittgenstein, *Philosophical Investigations*, 4th ed., eds. and trans. G. E. M. Anscombe, P. M. S. Hacker, and J. Schulte (Malden, MA: Blackwell, 2009 [1953]), 31d–32e.

14. See, e.g., Linda Nicholson, "Interpreting Gender," *Signs* 20, no. 1 (1994): 79–105; Natalie Stoljar, "Essence, Identity and the Concept of Woman," *Philosophical Topics* 23, no. 2 (1995): 261–94; Iris Marion Young, "Gender as Seriality: Thinking About Women as a Social Collective," in *Intersecting Voices* (Princeton: Princeton University Press, 1997); Linda Martín Alcoff, *Visible Identities: Race, Gender, and the Self* (Oxford: Oxford University Press, 2005); Ann Garry, "Intersectionality, Metaphors, and the Multiplicity of Gender," *Hypatia: A Journal of Feminist Philosophy* 26, no. 4 (2001): 826–50.

15. Frye, *Politics of Reality*, 40.

16. Nicholson, "Interpreting Gender," 96ff.

17. Will Roscoe, *Changing Ones: Third and Fourth Genders in Native North America* (New York: St. Martin's, 1998).

18. Ifi Amadiume, *Male Daughters, Female Husbands: Gender and Sex in an African Society* (London: Zed Books, 1987).

19. Gayatri Reddy, *With Respect to Sex: Negotiating Hijra Identity in South India* (Chicago: University of Chicago Press, 2005).

20. Anne Fausto-Sterling, *Sex/Gender: Biology in a Social World* (New York: Routledge, 1990).

21. See, e.g., Claire Ainsworth, "Sex Redefined: The Idea of 2 Sexes Is Overly Simplistic," *Nature*, February 2015, 18.

22. Lori Watson, "Feminist Perspectives on Human Nature," in *Macmillan Interdisciplinary Handbooks: Feminist Philosophy*, ed. Carol Hay (Farmington Hills, MI: Macmillan Reference USA, a part of Gale, Cengage Learning, 2017), 84.

23. Robin Dembroff, "Real Talk on the Metaphysics of Gender," *Gendered Oppression and Its Intersections*, an issue of *Philosophical Topics*, eds. Takaoka and Manna (forthcoming).

24. S. E. James, J. L. Herman, S. Rankin, M. Keisling, L. Mottet, and M. Anafi, *The Report of the 2015 U.S. Transgender Survey* (Washington, DC: National Center for Transgender Equality, 2016).

25. *LGBT in Britain: Hate Crime and Discrimination* (London: Stonewall, 2017).

26. "Violence Against the Transgender Community in 2018," Human Rights Campaign, accessed November 11, 2019, https://www.hrc.org/resources/violence-against-the-transgender-community-in-2018.

27. *LGBT in Britain.*

28. Tracy A. Becerra-Culqui, Yuan Liu, Rebecca Nash, Lee Cromwell, W. Dana Flanders, Darios Getahun, Shawn V. Giammattei, Enid M. Hunkeler, Timothy L. Lash, Andrea Millman, Virginia P. Quinn, Brandi Robinson, Douglas Roblin, David E. Sandberg, Michael J. Silverberg, Vin Tangpricha, and Michael Goodman, "Mental Health of Transgender and Gender Nonconforming Youth Compared with Their Peers," *Pediatrics* 141, no. 5 (2018).

29. Gemma L. Witcomb, Walter Pierre Bouman, Laurence Claes, Nicola Brewin, John R. Crawford, and Jon Arcelus, "Levels of Depression in Transgender People and Its Predictors: Results of a Large Matched Control Study with Transgender People Accessing Clinical Services," *Journal of Affective Disorders* 235, no. 1 (2018): 308–15.

30. Ann P. Haas, Philip L. Rodgers, and Jody L. Herman, "Suicide Attempts Among Transgender and Gender Non-Conforming Adults: Findings of the National Transgender Discrimination Survey," *American Foundation for Suicide Prevention and Williams Institute*, January 2014.

31. Jaclyn M. White Hughto and Sari L. Reisner, "A Systematic Review of the Effects of Hormone Therapy on Psychological Functioning and Quality of Life in Transgender Individuals," *Transgender Health* 1, no. 1 (2016): 21–31.

32. Janice Raymond, *The Transsexual Empire: The Making of the She-Male* (Boston: Beacon Press, 1979).

33. Raymond, *The Transsexual Empire*, 104.

34. Mary Daly, *Gyn/ecology: The Metaethics of Radical Feminism*, 2nd ed. (Boston: Beacon Press, 1990 [1978]), 70–71.

35. Raymond, *The Transsexual Empire*, 104.

36. Anonymous, "How the Michigan Womyn's Music Festival's Topless Womyn Changed My Lesbian Life Forever," *Autostraddle*, August 30, 2009, accessed November 11, 2019, https://www.autostraddle.com/how-the-michigan-womyns-music-festivals-topless-womyn-changed-my-lesbian-life-forever/.

37. Nancy Burkholder, interview by Cristan Williams, *The TransAdvocate*, April 9, 2013, accessed November 22, 2019, http://www.transadvocate.com/michigan-womyns-music-festival_n_8943.htm.

38. Lisa Vogel, "Letter from the Michigan Womyn's Music Festival," May 9, 2014, as cited in Sarah Gamble, "Gender and Transgender Criticism," in *Introducing Criticism in the 21st Century*, ed. Julian Wolfreys (Edinburgh: Edinburgh University Press, 2015).

39. Tobi Hill-Meyer, "Bitch Pulled from Festival Lineup," *Bilerico Report*, May 21, 2010, accessed November 11, 2019, http://bilerico.lgbtqnation.com/2010/05/bitch_pulled_from_festival_lineup.php; Rachel Carns, Radio Sloan, Dvin Kirakosian, Emily Kingan, STS, Tami Hart, "Response to Violence Against the Butchies and Le Tigre," *Eminism*, October 7, 2001, accessed November 11, 2019, http://eminism.org/michigan/20011007-carns.txt.

40. Chimamanda Ngozi Adichie, interview by Cathy Newman, *UK Channel 4 News*, March 20, 2017.

41. Caitlyn Jenner, interview by Kristin Harris, Whitney Jefferson, and Sydney Scott, BuzzFeed, November 10, 2015, accessed November 11, 2019, https://www.buzzfeed.com/kristinharris/caitlyn-jenner-the-power-of-the-woman-hasnt-been-unleashed.

42. Germaine Greer, interview by Kirsty Wark, *BBC Newsnight*, October 24, 2015.

43. Andrea Dworkin, *Woman-Hating* (New York: E. P. Dutton, 1974), 113–14. Emphasis in original.

44. Lori Watson, "The Woman Question," *Trans Studies Quarterly* 3 (2016): 246–53.

45. Jean-Paul Sartre, *Existentialism Is a Humanism*, trans. Carol Macomber (New Haven: Yale University Press, 2007 [1946]), 24–25.

46. Watson, "The Woman Question," 249.

47. Chimamanda Ngozi Adichie, Facebook post, March 10, 2017, accessed November 11, 2019, https://fr-fr.facebook.com/chimamandaadichie/posts/of-course-trans-women-are-part-of-feminism-i-do-not-believe-that-the-experience-/10154887462650944/.

48. Talia Mae Bettcher, "Evil Deceivers and Make-Believers: On Transphobic Violence and the Politics of Illusion," *Hypatia* 22, no. 3 (2007): 43–65.

49. Maren Behrensen, "Feminist Perspectives on LGBTQI Theory," in *Macmillan Interdisciplinary Handbooks: Feminist Philosophy*, ed. Carol Hay (Farmington Hills, MI: Macmillan Reference USA, a part of Gale, Cengage Learning, 2017), 345–48.

50. Talia Mae Bettcher, "Trans Identities and First-Person Authority," in *You've Changed: Sex Reassignment and Personal Identity*, ed. Laurie Shrage (New York: Oxford University Press, 2009).

51. Bettcher, "Trans Identities and First-Person Authority," 110.

52. Katharine Jenkins, "Amelioration and Inclusion: Gender Identity and the Concept of Woman," *Ethics* 126, no. 2 (2016): 394–421.

53. Julia Serano, *Whipping Girl: A Transsexual Woman on Sexism and the Scapegoating of Femininity*, 2nd ed. (Berkeley: Seal Press, 2016), 4.

CHAPTER 5: SEXUAL VIOLENCE

1. Catharine MacKinnon, *Feminism Unmodified* (Cambridge, MA: Harvard University Press, 1987), 171.

2. Rape, Abuse & Incest National Network, "Victims of Sexual Violence: Statistics," accessed November 11, 2019, https://www.rainn.org/get-information/statistics/sexual-assault-victims.

3. Robin Morgan, *Going Too Far: The Personal Chronicle of a Feminist* (New York: Random House, 1977), 163–64; Andrea Dworkin, *Pornography: Men Possessing Women* (New York: Penguin, 1989), 23; Susan Griffin, "Rape: The All-American Crime," *Ramparts* magazine, September 1971, 26–35.

4. Susan Brownmiller, *Against Our Will: Men, Women and Rape* (New York: Simon & Schuster, 1975), 15.

5. Ann J. Cahill, *Rethinking Rape* (Ithaca, NY: Cornell University Press, 2001).

6. William Blackstone, *Commentaries on the Laws of England* (Oxford: Clarendon Press, 1765), 430.

7. Brownmiller, *Against Our Will*, 209.

8. Andrea Dworkin, interview by Michael Sheldon, "I Was Taught to Be Too Nice to Boys," *Electronic Telegraph*, May 27, 2000, accessed November 11, 2019, http://fact.on.ca/news/news0005/te000527.htm.

9. Sandra Bartky, "On Psychological Oppression," *Femininity and Domination: Studies in the Phenomenology of Oppression* (New York: Routledge, 1990), 27.

10. Bartky, "On Psychological Oppression," 27.

11. Erving Goffman, *Behavior in Public Places* (New York: Free Press, 1963); and Erving Goffman, *Interaction Rituals* (New York: Pantheon, 1967).

12. Margaret Crouch, "Sexual Harassment in Public Places," *Social Philosophy Today* 25 (2009): 137–48.

13. Brownmiller, *Against Our Will*, 13–14.

14. Alison Jaggar, "Sex Inequality and Bias in Sex Differences Research," *Canadian Journal of Philosophy* 17 (1987): 36.

15. Cahill, *Rethinking Rape*, 23.

16. Catharine MacKinnon, "Pornography, Civil Rights, and Speech," *Harvard Civil Rights-Civil Liberties Law Review* 20, no. 1 (1985): 462.

17. MacKinnon, *Feminism Unmodified*, 34.

18. Morgan, *Going Too Far*, 169.

19. MacKinnon, *Feminism Unmodified*, 190.

20. MacKinnon, *Feminism Unmodified*, 187.

21. Abby Jackson, "The Frat Barred from Yale for 5 Years Is Back—and Women Are Saying They Warn One Another to Stay Away," *Business Insider*, January 25, 2018, accessed November 11, 2019, https://www.businessinsider.com/yale-delta-kappa-epsilon-2018-1.

22. Rae Langton, "Speech Acts and Unspeakable Acts," *Philosophy & Public Affairs* 22, no. 4 (1993): 293–330.

23. Langton, "Speech Acts," 299.

24. MacKinnon, *Feminism Unmodified*, 178.

25. Ellen Wills, "Lust Horizons: Is the Women's Movement Pro-Sex?," in

No More Nice Girls: Countercultural Essays (Minneapolis: University of Minnesota Press, 2012 [1981]), 3–14.

26. Gayle Rubin, "Thinking Sex: Notes for a Radical Theory of the Politics of Sexuality," in *Pleasure and Danger: Exploring Female Sexuality*, ed. Carole Vance (Boston: Routledge, 1984), 267–319.

27. Susie Bright, "The Feminist Sex Wars and the Myth of the Missing Middle," *Susie Bright's Journal*, March 13, 2013, accessed November 11, 2019, https://susiebright.blogs.com/susie_brights_journal_/2013/03/the-feminist-sex-wars-and-the-myth-of-the-missing-middle.html.

28. Whitney Strub, *Perversion for Profit: The Politics of Pornography and the Rise of the New Right* (New York: Columbia University Press, 2011).

29. Rape, Abuse & Incest National Network, "Statistics," accessed November 11, 2019, https://www.rainn.org/statistics.

30. Nancy Bauer, "Pornutopia," *n+1* 5 (2007): 70.

31. Bauer, "Pornutopia," 66.

32. Kelly Sue DeConnick, interview with Joshua Yehl, *IGN Comics*, June 20, 2013, accessed November 11, 2019, https://www.ign.com/articles/2013/06/20/kelly-sue-deconnick-talks-captain-marvel-pretty-deadly-and-the-sexy-lamp-test.

33. Linda LeMoncheck, "What's Wrong with Being a Sex Object?," in *Living with Contradictions: Controversies in Feminist Social Ethics*, ed. Alison Jaggar (Boulder: Westview Press, 1994), 199–206, and Linda LeMoncheck, "The Power of Sexual Stereotypes and the Sexiness of Power," in *Sexual Harassment: Issues and Answers*, eds. Linda LeMoncheck and James Sterba (New York: Oxford University Press, 2001), 264–69.

34. See, e.g., Bauer, "Pornutopia"; LeMoncheck, "What's Wrong with Being a Sex Object?"; and Martha Nussbaum, "Objectification," *Philosophy & Public Affairs* 24, no. 4 (1995): 249–91.

35. Bauer, "Pornutopia," 65.

36. Sandra Bartky, "Narcissism, Femininity, and Alienation," in *Femininity and Domination: Studies in the Phenomenology of Oppression* (New York: Routledge, 1990), 39.

37. See, e.g., Angela Harris, "Race and Essentialism in Feminist Legal Theory," *Stanford Law Review* 42, no. 3 (1990): 581–616; and Alison Stone, *An Introduction to Feminist Philosophy* (Malden, MA: Polity, 2007).

38. Harris, "Race and Essentialism."

39. Kate Manne, *Down Girl: The Logic of Misogyny* (New York: Oxford University Press, 2018), 33. Emphasis removed.

40. Daniel Silvermint, "Feminist Perspectives on Sexism and Oppression," in *Macmillan Interdisciplinary Handbooks: Feminist Philosophy*, ed. Carol Hay (Farmington Hills, MI: Macmillan Reference USA, a part of Gale, Cengage Learning, 2017), 37–70.

CHAPTER 6: WHERE THE RUBBER MEETS THE ROAD

1. Judith Lorber, *Paradoxes of Gender* (New Haven, CT: Yale University Press, 1994), 13.

2. John Stuart Mill, "The Subjection of Women," in John Stuart Mill and Harriet Taylor Mill, *Essays on Sex Equality*, ed. Alice Rossi (Chicago: University of Chicago Press, 1970 [1869]), 27.

3. Mill, "Subjection of Women," 27.

4. Ruth Whippman, "Enough Leaning in, Let's Tell Men to Lean Out," *The New York Times*, October 10, 2019, accessed November 11, 2019, https://www.nytimes.com/2019/10/10/opinion/sunday/feminism-lean-in.html?searchResultPosition=2.

5. Simone de Beauvoir, *The Second Sex*, ed. and trans. H. M. Parshley (New York: Vintage, 1989 [1949]), xxv.

6. de Beauvoir, *The Second Sex*, 663.

7. Bethany Saltman, interview with Samantha Stark, *The New York Times*, April 8, 2018, accessed November 11, 2019, https://www.nytimes.com/2018/04/08/insider/antioch-sexual-consent-form-metoo-video.html.

8. Jessica Valenti and Jaclyn Friedman, *Yes Means Yes: Visions of Female Sexual Power* (Berkeley: Seal Press, 2008), 9.

9. Rebecca Kukla, "Sex Talks," *Aeon*, February 4, 2019, accessed November 11, 2019, https://aeon.co/essays/consent-and-refusal-are-not-the-only-talking-points-in-sex. Also see Rebecca Kukla, "That's What She Said: The Language of Sexual Negotiation," *Ethics* 129 (2018): 70–97.

10. Julia Serano, *Whipping Girl: A Transsexual Woman on Sexism and the Scapegoating of Femininity*, 2nd ed. (Berkeley: Seal Press, 2016), 3.

11. Mike Woods, online petition, December 28, 2014, accessed November 11, 2019, https://www.thestar.com/news/gta/2014/12/28/manspreading_a_transit_controversy_with_legs.html.

12. Ash Bennington and Mark Skinner, "Manspreading: The Myth & The

Math (Dude)," *Economonitor,* accessed November 11, 2019, https://moneymaven.io/economonitor/us/manspreading-the-myth-the-math-dude-seXorYaLiEOvigtPToazvw/.

13. Bonnie Mann, "Creepers, Flirts, Heroes, and Allies: Four Theses on Sexual Harassment," *APA Newsletter on Feminism and Philosophy* 11, no. 2 (2012): 24–31.

14. Mann, "Creepers, Flirts, Heroes, and Allies," 24.

15. Mann, "Creepers, Flirts, Heroes, and Allies," 13.

16. Mann, "Creepers, Flirts, Heroes, and Allies," 27.

17. Sandra Bartky, "Feminine Masochism and the Politics of Personal Transformation," in *Femininity and Domination: Studies in the Phenomenology of Oppression* (New York: Routledge, 1990), 52.

18. Bartky, "Feminine Masochism," 52.

19. Bartky, "Feminine Masochism," 60.

20. Audre Lorde, speech at Harvard University, 1982, accessed November 11, 2019, https://www.blackpast.org/african-american-history/1982-audre-lorde-learning-60s/.

INDEX